D1635068

THE WOMAN WITH NINE LIVES

Going Forward, Stepping Back

Iby Knill

A sequel to the best-selling
The Woman Without a Number

Scratching Shed Publishing Ltd

Cover: Iby Knill, pictured in 1947
Back: Iby and Frank Gardner, Kaunitz, 2010;
ID card, September 1946

Typeset in Warnock Pro Semi Bold and Palatino
Printed and bound in the United Kingdom by
Latimer Trend & Company Ltd,
Estover Road, Plymouth, PL6 7PY

To my father Beno (Benjy), for imbuing me with a love of music and books and for his gentleness, and my mother, the incredible Irene, and her immense capacity for living, taking risks and energy.

And finally to Bert, my late husband, for his patience, quiet understanding, quirky sense of humour and loving support without which I would not have survived and been able to stand up for myself.

Acknowledgements

This has not been an easy book to write. As much had to be left out as has been written, thoughts had to be given to people who were involved in my life but who would not necessarily like to have details publicised, so there are hidden stories here.

Profound thanks are due to Tracy Craggs to whom large chunks of the books were dictated and who heard, with compassion, the parts which have been omitted. She was a continuous help in sorting, copying, chivvying me along and, last but not least, sitting beside me through numerous skype interviews.

Thanks also to the Holocaust Survivors Friendship Association for their generous support and to Scott Flaving.

Contents

Foreword

Fabian Hamilton MP

*

I HAVE been Iby's local MP for more than 18 years but I only met her for the first time about six years ago.

I saw her on the BBC's *My Story* series, found out where she lived and managed to get hold of her phone number from a mutual friend.

I asked whether I could come and meet her and she agreed, so one Friday when I was back in the constituency I went round to see her and heard much of her history first hand. I was struck with how articulate she was, as well as the humour she used in telling her riveting odyssey. Her poems are beautifully written too.

Iby is an extraordinary person. In just telling me what had happened to her I was transported back in time, so vivid was her memory. Frank Gardner's BBC film, with Iby narrating, was fascinating, but hearing her in person was even more compelling.

I'd visited Auschwitz Birkenau before, so it was easier

to imagine the description of her life there, but what was so amazing was her insistence that as long as she and her group of women who ended up in the camp in 1944 stuck together, then they would be harder to pick off individually – and it clearly worked.

I don't know how anyone could keep such a terrifying and traumatic part of her life inside her head for so long, but when she decided to tell the tale, it came pouring out. Her book, *The Woman Without a Number*, was just the first episode, beautifully told in clear English, which is not even her first (or second) language.

Iby seems to defy age and time. When you listen to her talking about her experience up to the time of her arrest and of her period inside the camps, it really is as if you are there yourself.

Now in her early 90s, she still gives talks and lectures all over the UK and, via technology, abroad. It's as if she cannot rest until all of humanity has heard what she has to tell. After I met her for the first time in 2010, I asked whether she would consider doing a lecture in the Speaker's Rooms in the House of Commons.

When I met with the Speaker, John Bercow, a few weeks later, he was deeply moved by Iby's story and arranged for her to come as his guest and speak to MPs, Peers and staff in his State Apartments at the Palace of Westminster.

So riveting is her style, even though The Speaker had another engagement, he stayed to listen to everything Iby had to say and then rose to give her his personal thanks for coming.

I've met Iby many times over the years since and we correspond regularly. My admiration for her increases after every conversation and I hope that she is able to carry on her vital work for as long as she can because we all need to be reminded every day not only of the horrors of the Holocaust, but of how the human spirit can overcome the evil that humanity is capable of by replacing it with loving kindness, forgiveness and friendship, of which I believe Iby to be the embodiment.

Fabian Hamilton MP
House of Commons
January 2016

Introduction

❊

WHEN I was about eight years old, in Bratislava, there was a fashion for autograph books. I presented mine to my German teacher who wrote in it, 'What you do, do well: it is better to do nothing than do things badly.' Then my English teacher added, 'If at first you don't succeed, try, try again!'

I found it really difficult to get those two statements to reconcile.

The first one appeared to me to say leave things I could not do to those who could, but the second was quite another matter. I wondered was this the difference between the German and English attitude to life?

It was not until much later that I realised that I had misconstrued the German proverb. What it really meant was: when it comes to taking action, do what is right; it is better not to do anything rather than to do evil, and for a long time what was the governing principle in my life: do no evil.

Yet, I started to wonder, as my sphere of experience widened, what about standing by and doing nothing when somebody else does something evil? Is that not tantamount to being complicit? The boundaries blurred.

I never counted the fact that I was involved in the underground movement helping downed Allied aircrew to escape as an action coming under the heading of doing right; it was just something I got involved in, unintentionally, but with dire consequences.

After my cousin who I was staying with was called up to the military, I was hidden by a solicitor and his wife. He was involved in the group which helped bailed out airmen make their way from German-occupied countries through Greece to Crete, where there was still a British presence. It was my job to meet them, there were usually two, and pass them on to others who would help them on their way.

Unfortunately, somehow the movement was betrayed, all 428 of us were arrested and we were interrogated, quite forcibly. Being an illegal immigrant with false papers I was particularly vulnerable but I only knew members of my cell.

I was sent to the women's prison in Budapest, where the interrogation continued. The Hungarian government decided, eventually, not to prosecute us. I was released but immediately re-arrested as an illegal immigrant and spent nearly two years in detention centres and refugee camps.

Shortly after my release on parole in March 1944, the Nazis occupied Hungary and I finished up in a brickyard and then, on 17 June 1944, in Auschwitz-Birkenau. I left Auschwitz after volunteering to do slave labour as a nurse.

It was when I was in charge of the hospital at the Lippstadt slave labour camp that I actively and purposefully tried to take the 'right' action.

There were 780 women in the camp. According to the Nazis' strict rules there could never be more than half a per cent ill and in hospital. Epidemics of contagious diseases and work accidents were no excuse for exceeding the magic number of 38 patients.

But there were occasions when we had fewer patients than that. People worked 12-hour shifts day and night, and some got so exhausted they would have been liable to accidents or lessened productivity.

Wherever possible I tried to manufacture a few days' rest for them to ensure they were not seen as a liability and 'dispensed' with. It was an open secret how to manipulate the thermometer and give a bogus high reading. And we also managed to hide the three woman who had given birth there and who were breastfeeding their babies. But it was not always possible to take in all who needed or demanded it.

One of those I assisted told the commandant what I was doing. The next day I was accused of 'sabotaging the war effort' and, no longer in charge of the hospital, put on the 12-hour night shift in the factory on the heaviest machinery.

Actually, that gave me more opportunity to sabotage the war effort. Tolerance levels on machine gun bullets were low and I somewhat managed to exceed them nearly continually, my excuse being that I had no experience in this sort of work so what could they expect.

Fortunately for all of us, supplies of iron to the factory stopped and we were put on a march to Bergen-Belsen. We never arrived there, we were liberated by Allied troops on 1 April 1945.

Thinking about what my German teacher wrote and talking about it to my children has actually thrown up many conundrums. Obviously, if it is you alone, you can stand up, speak up and act accordingly but what do you do when you are a mother and your children's life and safety depend on you? Would you sacrifice them? Do you have the right to do so?

Even with what I have seen and learned, I don't have an answer. In the end, it is up to each and every one of us to decide and to live with the consequences of our actions or complicity.

*****

I WASN'T really sure how to end my first book, *The Woman Without a Number* or even where to start this one. It had always been my intention, once I began writing my memoir, to split my life into two parts; that before 1947 and what has happened to me since coming to England.

The first book was not a chronology, it ended at the beginning, explaining what our family from Czechoslovakia lost – had taken - not just possessions, but each other.

When I came to begin piecing this volume together, I suddenly realised that there were so many different parts to it.

It struck me why I adore cats. Like them, I appear to have had nine lives.

Tomy's Story

✻

After the Prague Spring in 1968, Tomy visited us. He wanted to tell me his story and for me to translate it into English because he wanted others to know about it. A German translation was published in the *Viennese Jewish Chronicle* in 1999.

My brother was born in Bratislava on 19 January 1929 and passed away in the year 2000. These are his words.

IT was summer 1944 and Budapest was experiencing the penultimate year of the horrors of the Second World War. We couldn't know how long it would be before victory over fascism but we felt that the tyranny could not last much longer. Our biggest worry was not knowing what we could possibly do to survive.

A year earlier I'd come, together with my parents, cousin and grandmother, illegally from Slovakia to Budapest, where we were placed in an internment camp as Jewish immigrants.

We, being too young, and my grandmother too old, were later released but my parents had to stay there.

The Hungarian regime wanted to show how efficient they were, how many Jews they had already managed to send 'to work' in Auschwitz.

Each day there in spring 1944 was the same. In the morning, there was an air raid by American planes which made the very air tremble and in the evening the Russians came over to bomb Budapest, admittedly not in such a great number nor did they inflict as much damage.

If the wind was in the right direction, you could also hear the noise of the ongoing battles on the eastern front. What was a fearful sound for most people was, for us, even more beautiful than a symphony by Beethoven, it signalled salvation might be on its way.

In June 1944, my parents were transported 'to work' at Auschwitz. At the station I wanted to join them but my father shouted to me that I should get away and go either to the Swiss or the Swedish embassy, either of which was bound to help me.

A Hungarian gendarme standing nearby, who was supposed to supervise the transportation, turned round and also shouted: 'Get away, before it is too late.'

Heavy-heartedly I left, not realising that this would be the last time I saw my father. He and the gendarme saved my life. Father threw his knotted handkerchief to me in which he had put his golden watch chain.

I went to the Swedish embassy in Gyopar Street, where the ambassador Mr. Danielson was just about to leave. His driver, Mr. Toth, came from Palarikovo in Slovakia (which at that time was part of Hungary). He stopped the car and asked me what I wanted.

I told him the truth; I had nowhere to stay, my parents

had been taken away, I was a Jew from Slovakia, was looking for somewhere to sleep and that I was willing to do any kind of work.

Mr Toth told the Ambassador: 'Let's take the poor lad in, we'll find something for him to do.' The Ambassador agreed and told me to wait until he came back. I slept in the bottom of the lift shaft, washed cars, took mail to the post office, anything I was asked to do.

I was happy that I had a place to rest, something to eat and also got a pass from the Hungarian Foreign Office stating that I was a member of the Swedish embassy.

I had the advantage that, thanks to my parents, I spoke not only Slovak but also German like a native and also reasonable Hungarian.

In July 1944, the secretary at the Embassy, Mrs. Brigit, called me and asked me to go with Mr. Toth in the official car to the railway station to meet a new envoy.

The station was in a frightful state, half the buildings had been destroyed in air raids, it was swarming with soldiers, refugees and members of the Hungarian Fascist organisation 'Nyilas' in uniform, who were engaged in trying to identify any Jews.

On the way back, the new man, Mr. Wallenberg, asked me who I was and what I was doing at the Embassy. I told him truthfully how I had got there and what my role was. He proposed that I should help him in his mission and, although I didn't know what it was, I agreed. Our first contact was positive and very friendly.

The embassy rented a villa next to it in Minerva Street and Mr. Wallenberg lived and worked there. I continued to sleep at the bottom of the lift shaft of the main building but went every morning to his house and worked there until the evening.

I acted as doorkeeper, admitted people, took care of the mail and turned my hand to whatever was required. Mr. Wallenberg did not know Budapest, so I frequently accompanied him into town and waited for him in the car until he had done his business. Each evening I went to the post office to send coded telegrams to Sweden. The code of the embassy consisted of groups of five letters, the military attaché's code was a number, which is all I can remember about it.

After a time there was a change in the type of caller who came to us. The embassy started to issue 'safe passes' in the traditional Swedish yellow colour to Jewish people.

The document was proof that the bearer was under the protection of the Swedish crown. They were issued within 24 hours of application and looked official. People who had these passes were accommodated in so-called Swedish houses within the ghetto.

The rooms showed the Swedish flag, had been furnished by Mr. Wallenberg and this was often a successful ruse.

Officially, the condition for the issue of these passes was that the applicant had a relative living in Sweden but nobody checked or asked what the actual relationship was.

For people who had no such family, I had the telephone books of Stockholm and other Swedish towns from which people could 'find' one.

Mr. Wallenberg had given me these phone books with strict instructions. He was certain that I would be able to spot an agent provocateur and told me to be very careful; if there were any problems I was to drop them into the letter box next to the entrance of the embassy.

Now I was only seldom in the town, as we spent day and night producing the documentation.

I had an oval stamp, issued by the Embassy and, in case an applicant had no photo, a box full of passport-sized ones and picked one of the right gender and age and glued it on.

Later on, Mr. Wallenberg's operation moved into a building near the castle and then eventually to the other side of the Danube, to Illoi Street 2.

Here the section grew with new collaborators and all the employees – all of them Jews – slept in the offices so that they would not be exposed to the risk of being caught on the streets.

Contacts with official personnel, Hungarians as well as Germans, continued in the Minerva Street embassy so that the size of the 'Wallenberg Section' should not become common knowledge.

IN the autumn of 1944 transports to Auschwitz ceased but they went now in a westerly direction and left Hungary at Sopron. I heard that my 60-year-old aunt, Bella, was in one of them. Instantly I made out a safety pass for her and assuming that her train had not yet left Hungary, I got on to my motorbike and rode to Sopron.

There I went to the gendarme headquarters, where I found armed members of Nyilas were also supervising the deportations. Without giving it a second thought, I showed them my own pass, which proved that I was a member of the Swedish embassy and gave them my aunt's safety documents.

Since my Hungarian was heavily accented, I must have given them the right impression when I asked them to send my aunt immediately back to Budapest. I was successful! I put her into a Swedish safe house where she survived and saw Hungary liberated.

One day, Mr. Wallenberg told me that under no circumstances was I to go Minerva Street as an important visitor was expected, who should not see me under any circumstances. He arrived in the evening; it was Adolf Eichmann.

AT the beginning of November 1944, when we could all hear the sound of gunfire from the approaching front, all members of the Swedish embassy packed their suitcases and drove back, through Germany, to Sweden.

To my great surprise Mr. Wallenberg did not go with them. He told me that his mission had not yet been completed. An appendix was added to my Swedish pass which until now was in Swedish, German and Hungarian.

It was in Russian and stated: 'To be used only for crossing the border.' At the beginning of December, Mr. Wallenberg moved into the flat of a Hungarian family in the castle which had direct access to its underground bunkers. From then, until the Germans left, he did not come into the embassy any more.

At the end of December, Russian troops started to enter the city. On 19th January they liberated the left side of the town, Pest, but the withdrawing German forces demolished all the bridges across the Danube. On 12th February, 1945 the Russian troops liberated Buda.

I started to look everywhere for Mr. Wallenberg, without success. Everybody just shook their heads, nobody had seen him. On 26th February three Russian staff cars drew up in front of the Swedish embassy.

It was pure chance that I was there but it gave me the opportunity to see everything. High ranking Russian officers got out of the car and behind them Mr. Wallenberg in his usual long coat and wide hat.

Raoul Wallenberg spoke to the officers through an interpreter. He declared something and pointed to both buildings of the embassy. The whole thing seemed to me dream-like, unreal. As I approached them and was about to speak to Mr. Wallenberg, he indicated behind his back with his hand, that I should go away and said: 'Schlecht – verschwinde' (It's bad, get away!)

Then they all got into the cars and nobody in Hungary ever saw him again.

I had no idea what had happened in front of me. How can a man be persecuted who saved so many from certain death, who had organised the Swedish houses in the ghetto of Budapest, who never showed any fear of Eichmann? We were free, we had survived but I could not understand this world.

The next day I left Budapest and rode to Kosice where I volunteered for the Czechoslovak Army. I wanted to have a weapon in my hands to liberate my country, find my family and destroy all the sources of the hated fascist murders. I was just 16-years-old.

It wasn't until years later, when I returned to Bratislava in May 1945, that the facts hit me.

My mother had returned from the concentration camp but not my father who had been murdered in November 1944 in the gas chambers of Auschwitz, on the last occasion they were used.

Tomy, pictured in 1947

Life One

*

The time in the camps had, obviously, an effect on our overall health. After liberation they diagnosed that I, like many others, had a touch of tuberculosis but it cleared up.

We all suffered from diseases of the gums, our teeth were either loose or many had had them pulled out and finished up, prematurely, with dentures.

I had no fillings and was determined to keep my teeth, even if it meant that for many months I had to eat very carefully and my gums bled frequently.

But worse than all that were the boils, which we all had agonized over and continued to suffer from for many months after liberation.

It must have been at least six months later, in the winter of 1945, when a lump appeared on the left side of my neck. I assumed that it was just another boil, but the lump just got bigger without coming to a head.

I was averse to consulting a German doctor, so went over to Bielefeld hospital where one of our doctors was now working. The lump was removed but a few weeks later another one formed there and grew at an alarming rate. A biopsy showed malignancy. Under a general anaesthetic the lump and the underlying tissue, including part of my thyroid gland, was removed.

When I returned to Bratislava, further tests were carried out and I was told that there were still some malignant cells present and that radium therapy was required. I was informed that there was likely to be burns left on the site, so I decided to wait until after my wedding.

The treatment, at this time, consisted of the direct application of radium. A small container was fashioned, I think of lead, of a size to cover the site, into which were placed some thin rods of radium.

A covering of cork went over it and the contraption was fixed with a bandage to my neck, initially for two hours.

The next week this was increased to four hours and the number of rods added to, then to eight hours. I cannot remember how many treatments were given. The whole area reddened and the central part looked like a deep burn wound.

By the time I came to England this had more or less healed, but the scar remained with me. However the treatment was successful and there was no recurrence. My thyroid gland ceased to function altogether a few years later and for the rest of my life I have had to take thyroid tablets.

1947

ON 17th March, 1947, I arrived in Britain and was joined on the following day by my husband Bert, back from military duties in Germany. The War Office had posted him back to Cornwall.

Bert had been instructed to report to the Duke of Cornwall's Light Infantry depot in Bodmin; I was to stay with Doll and Will, his sister and brother-in-law in Bristol, get acquainted with Stuart – Bert's son from his first marriage - who lived with them, and, perhaps, get down soon to Cornwall.

Bert's house in Truro was let until June, otherwise it would have been requisitioned. Empty houses were a no-no.

DOLL and Will lived in a council house in Staple Hill. To me, the streets looked alike, all the houses had privet hedges of the same height which divided the small front gardens from the pavement. It was just after the war and uniformity still ruled.

I got continually lost, had to return to the nearest main road and then work my way back from there.

Theirs was quite big for a council house; it had four bedrooms, three of them doubles, and a bathroom with an asthmatic geyser for hot water. The front door, which was never used, led in to a square entrance hall and a parlour with a plush maroon sofa, a small table and chairs and a piano with two candleholders.

The piano was very much out of tune yet Doll, who boasted of having had ten lessons, loved to accompany the Sunday sing-songs they liked with gusto, frequently hitting the wrong keys.

Harmony was accidental rather than intentional. That the sour notes, hit with great assurance and force and more-or-less three quarter tones down, visibly shook me and set my teeth on edge was, I hoped, not too noticeable.

Bert also had a good ear and could play the piano but, for reasons I never discovered, preferred only the black notes.

I was also invited to perform but managed to avoid it

saying, quite truthfully, that I could only play with music in front of me and my books had not yet arrived.

I THINK I must have upset the applecart on my first day at Doll and Will's. At home, in Hungary and in Czechoslovakia, it was common practice in the morning to open the bedroom window and spread out your bedding on the windowsill and chairs by it to air, so I did just that.

The horror of it! The consternation when they realized what I had done!

In England, you kept the window shut to keep the moist air out and re-made your bed quickly so as to prevent the all-pervading dampness chilling you to the bone when you went to sleep at night.

Naturally, there was no heating in the bedrooms. A stone hot water bottle was inserted into the bed a couple of hours before you retired to remove, hopefully, any vestiges of moisture which could have insinuated themselves under the layers of grey blankets.

I was used to feather-beds made from Hungarian goose down, the lightest, finest and warmest in the world. Here, the blankets were really heavy and Bert wrapped himself into more than his fair share of them.

As a child I was used to a quick hot bath in the morning. With one bathroom and hot water only from the temperamental geyser and Doll, Will, their daughters Renee and Margaret, Stuart, Bert and myself in the house, this was not possible.

When the call came that breakfast was ready, I was not, and I was not going to get dressed without a bath or at least a proper wash. So I put on my lovely pink silk negligee, part of my trousseau, around the lower edge of which I had painted Chinese characters in shades of blue and jade green and sailed down into the living room with its big square table, around which sat the others, all properly dressed, who looked at me open-mouthed.

At home, we often breakfasted on a weekend, in dressing gowns, but not here. Coming downstairs in a nightie, however well covered, was just not decent. Not a good beginning.

THE living room was the hub of the house. Its fireplace was flanked on one side by a display case, we used to call it a vitrine, in which the best glass and china was displayed. On the other side was a cabinet with the radio on it. There were two armchairs either side of the fireplace, a small settee under the window, the square table with six chairs and a sideboard.

One door led into the hallway, the other into the kitchen.

A porcelain sink with a wooden draining board, dresser with a metal surface, a table, gas cooker and a boiler for washing clothes furnished the kitchen. A pantry opened off it and another door led to a covered porch with a door to the coal shed.

The path beside the house led to a shed and to the garden at the back, where the previous lawn had been converted into a vegetable patch. I had no idea what a lawn was. The garden was quite big and there were bushes of soft fruit at the bottom and I seem to remember also rabbit hutches and possibly a chicken run.

The house was cold. There was a fireplace in the living room and this was lit first thing in the morning during these early spring days. There was also a small one in the parlour but it was only fired if it was going to be used, and that was rarely.

Hot water, except for the geyser in the bathroom

which only heated the bath water, came from a kettle in the kitchen so Will shaved in there, as did most working men in those days.

AMERICAN fashions and ideas had come over with the GIs and the Marshall Plan. One of them was the 'university settlement movement'.

The idea was to create centres in housing estates to provide the residents with a focal point, a place for youngsters to go after school to play table tennis - still called ping-pong at that time, to encourage wives to meet for talks on wider topics than merely domestic ones and to promote the development of crafts; in essence, to make a community out of an estate.

Near the allotments at Staple Hill, not far from Will's home, there was a derelict building and students from Bristol University set about making it useable. They went round the houses asking for help, from the men for its construction and anyone who had other skills and knowledge to share.

This was a God-send to me. Before long I spent most of my afternoons there, first whitewashing freshly plastered walls then giving talks to the women's group on life in post-war Europe, on the theme of 'how to ensure peace in the future' which, looking back, was extremely brave. Even before I started speaking the knitting came out, the needles began clicking and it went on until the tea came.

I played table-tennis with the youngsters, taught them volleyball, anything I could do. It was fun and it kept me productively occupied.

A few years ago I drove past the site of the settlement and it is now a thriving, permanent, all-purpose community centre, so our seeds fell on fertile ground.

Will could not understand it at all. Why was I doing

it? Wasn't there enough to be occupied with in the house to keep a woman busy? Doll didn't mind, she often came with me but being quiet while someone else talked was very difficult for her.

AT the time, Will was an engine fireman with the Great Western Railway, the train line between Penzance and Paddington. Firing the engines was hard, arduous work and required a lot of energy.

All food was rationed but heavy manual workers like Will got an extra allowance of protein in the form of cheese.

There was only so much of it a man could stomach and he was small and wiry so cheese was frequently used also in the family meals, usually in the shape of a sauce on cauliflower or as a Welsh rarebit. The cheese was bog-standard cheddar, mousetrap stuff and, just occasionally, there was processed cheese from America which felt and tasted like rubber.

When Will had married Doll – Dorothy – in 1930, he was in the Navy but she did not relish the life of a sailor's wife so he left and joined the railway. He rose through the ranks and was now studying to become an engine driver, the dream of so many little boys then.

These were steam trains and he would tell you at length about the refinements required in firing so that the engine had enough steam for the steep sections and low pressure on the declines.

One train crew did not do the whole run, shifts were long and arduous. He was now studying diesel engines, which were due to be introduced on the line.

Will's hobby was first aid. He had been a member of St. John Ambulance for many years and reached the highest levels of proficiency, eventually being made a Knight of St.

John the greatest honour in the service, receiving it from the King at Buckingham Palace, the high point of his life.

Will's two daughters ran rings around him, and Doll hardly ever stopped talking. She got even worse after his death, if that was possible. But then, continuous talking and not listening was a Knill trait and only Bert didn't have it, the army probably knocked it out of him.

WILL had no idea about how to cope with boys and Stuart had had a pretty tough deal by the time he came to live with him and Doll, aged six or seven. Win, Bert's first wife and Stuart's mother, appears to have been ailing from shortly after he was born.

By the time he was three, she was diagnosed, belatedly, with breast cancer. Initially, the doctor thought that the lump was due to impact from the handle of a fork when she had been gardening. When they eventually operated they had to remove both breasts and also the lymphatic glands.

Stuart went first to stay with Win's half-sister and her family in Parr in Cornwall, but the arrangement did not work out satisfactorily. I never found out why. Win then came up to Bristol for treatment and Stuart came with her.

They lived with Elaine, Bert's brother Harry's wife, who had been a nurse, while Harry was away in the army. Win was very ill and did not think that the sickroom was the right environment for Stuart.

Bert was now in Pevensey with the forces preparing for the D-Day landings but he was allowed home on compassionate leave.

Bert thought that Frank and Connie, Stuart's godparents, would be best suited to look after him, especially as Connie had been a teacher, but Win wanted Stuart to be with a family who had children rather than just with a woman as Frank was also enlisted. Win insisted that Stuart should go and live with Doll and Will.

Because of his job, Will was exempt from military service, and they did have two children, albeit girls.

Renee, the eldest, was about to leave school and start work in an office, but Margaret was only two or three years older than Stuart. However, that age gap was significant and Margaret did not like the idea of a boy coming into the family and treated him cruelly.

Will thought that boys had to be brought up tough and Stuart wasn't settled at school either, his third different one; it was an extremely difficult environment for him.

He was a lonely, disturbed child, his father away, mother seriously ill and nobody even trying to understand what he was going through.

I tried to assure him that things would be different, better, once the school year was over and we had moved back to Cornwall.

His elder brother of ten years, Peter, had been adopted by Bert and Win when he was just a few days old. He was very bright and a high-flying student at Truro Grammar School but Win's illness put a stop to his ambitions too.

When she had to go to Bristol for treatment, Peter was left isolated. He was, by then, a member of the school's army cadet force and aged 15, was accepted at the Army Apprentice School at Arborfield to train as an armourer.

Bert took him by train and on the way disclosed that he had been adopted, as he would have to hand over the necessary certificate when enrolling.

Not only was Peter torn from his secure family surroundings and the school where he had excellent prospects, and concerned about the mother who had brought him up being seriously ill in hospital, but now his sense of identity was in question.

Much later, Bert told me who Peter's birth parents were. I don't know whether he ever told him.

Many years later, Peter – who called himself Dave from the moment he left home – told me that he hadn't really wanted to go to Arborfield. He could have stayed at Truro school and boarded with friends but that his mother had decided he should have the safety of the army. He was never told what the matter with his mother was. Cancer was not something people mentioned then and he had no idea she was so ill.

When Win died in October 1944, Peter was called to the unit orderly room, told about her passing and given a travel warrant to Bristol to attend her funeral. He went to Will and Doll's, where Stuart now lived. Bert had arrived from Germany. Peter refused to believe that his adopted mother had died and would not to go to the funeral. Bert was angry and couldn't understand or forgive that and he never did. Nobody tried to understand what Peter was going through or offered to help him.

CORNWALL

Come April 1947, Bert was in the Duke of Cornwall's Light Infantry depot in Bodmin and from there he was sent to act as a recruiting officer in St. Austell. He found lodgings with a widowed lady in Highertown and, after a few weeks, asked me to come down for a fortnight to have a look at the area.

The train from Bristol went all along the coast, the sun shone on the sea and the banks of rhododendrons along the track were in full bloom. I had never seen such gorgeous flowers before, it seemed a wonderful, different world. When

Bert told me that rhododendrons grew wild in China I thought it was just another of his tall stories.

I found Cornwall enchanting, from the white china-clay pyramids in the south to the breakers at Newquay on the northern coast, from Marazion and its gull-encircled fishing boats, St. Michael's Mount, to the miles of white expanse of Praa sands; I had never seen anything like it. I fell in love with the place. The railway took me everywhere and I walked miles.

Cornish cuisine was a different matter. Admittedly, rationing was still on but here milk was plentiful, as was fish of all sorts. I made reluctant acquaintance with junket and a watery liquid called gravy which accompanied every kind of meat, whatever its cut and however it had been cooked.

I had a surfeit of pilchards in every possible form, from tinned ones in tomato sauce – which I remembered from Germany – to star-gazy pie, where the heads with their milky eyes looked out at you from the edge while the tails stood to attention in the middle, not an alluring sight.

I also tried several varieties of Cornish pasty. I was assured that they were not the authentic ones because they could not get the right kind of meat, it had to be skirt of beef. They also claimed that only Cornish women could make them properly but I learned and mine are acknowledged to be amongst the best!

We did not go to look at Bert's house in Truro. He thought it best that I should see it when I took it over. In the meantime, I went back to Doll's and again tried to find out whether there was any way I could fit in.

EVENTUALLY the day came when the tenants moved out of Bert's house, Viview, in Hendra Barton, named so because it faced a huge viaduct which spanned a section of Truro, at the end of which was the railway station. At night you could hear the drivers shouting to each other as they shunted the engines about.

Most people thought that the house was named after me because Bert's family and army friends called me Vi, short for Violet, but it had been chosen by Win – sheer coincidence.

Sister-in-law Elaine came down with me to put the place to rights. One bedroom had been kept locked and Bert had put all their bedding, bed linen and table linen in there. The house had been let to a naval officer, his wife and young child. Naturally, they had not done anything to the large garden.

On arrival, we tried to get the front gate open but couldn't. We went round to the side along the three feet high wall and could see why. Everything was overgrown and the path itself was hidden under waist-high grass. The drive at the side was clear and from there we circled the house and found that we could get in by the back door.

A short passage led to the kitchen. An unpleasant smell greeted us; partially cleaned pots and pans lay on the wooden draining board. From the kitchen into the hall, the dining room on the right, then the door into the sitting room. Wallpaper hung off the walls, a radiogram lay on its side on the floor. Turning left toward the stairs, woodworm holes were evident in the staircase panelling.

Upstairs, the two front bedrooms were more or less alright, the back one passable. Taking out Bert's key and opening the fourth, smallest bedroom, where the linen and some best china should have been in the built-in cupboards, there was hardly anything.

Half a dozen sheets, a few army blankets, a handful of towels, a few dishes; the mystery of where the rest and most valuable stuff had gone was never solved. I told Bert not to worry as mine was on its way. Rationing was still in force and linen and clothing could only be obtained with coupons. A newly-wed couple got an allocation but, as Bert had been married before, we did not qualify.

Elaine stayed for a week. We set about cleaning and scrubbing, pulling off the remnants of wallpaper, the damp having already done most of the work, and painting everything in the only available colours magnolia and white gloss woodwork.

I asked Bert which had been his and Win's bedroom and told him that, if he didn't mind – and even if he did – we would sleep in the other one until my own furniture arrived.

Most of the pots and pans had rusted and had to be thrown out but we brought the remainder of the nice bone china down and proceeded to use it until I managed to get some traditional Cornish pottery for the kitchen. I think I still have a couple of flat platters in cream with pale blue and gold rims.

I had never liked housework and was not going to change. I would cook, preserve fruit, paint, decorate and spring-clean but day-to-day dusting was not my forte. So Mrs. Minter came in twice a week to help out.

Jimmy Eva, Bert's batman, also did his share and the gardening. Just as well, as neither Bert nor I had done any before. However, the first things which needed attention were the cracks between the windows and the woodworm in the staircase.

A builder came and explained that there were two problems, both equally urgent. The cracks were due to dry weather and a shifting of the foundations as sea-sand had been used in the construction, which had attracted moisture. We were innocent as babes-in-arms, he could have told us anything and we would have believed it.

He told us that the foundations needed underpinning and then the gaps could be filled with 'proper mortar' and it might be possible to re-use the window frames, but he was not certain about it. The repairs cost nearly as much as Bert had paid for the house before the war.

After that, it was a question of the woodworm; he wanted to replace the whole structure although there was damage only to the side panels. I told him we would think about it as I had an idea that, perhaps, it could be solved in another way.

I then discovered that there was also woodworm in the back panel of the upright piano. First things first, the house had to be saved but so had the piano, I could not live without it.

Mrs. Minter said she knew a piano tuner. He duly came and told me to get a liquid to spray into all the worm holes. A lengthy business but it saved the piano as well as the panels of the staircase, which did not need replacing after all.

The woodworm had not migrated into the stairs, as we discovered when we carefully inspected the underside from the cupboard underneath them. Since at home in Bratislava all stairs were made of stone or concrete and walls of bricks which did not shift, I learned quite a bit about building methods in Britain and was not impressed.

I then went back to Bristol to pick up Stuart at the end of the school year.

BERT had been transferred back with the rank of major, as quartermaster, but we knew that it was not a permanent posting, his original, similar role having been with the 5th Battalion, which had been disbanded.

Almost all military personnel had, by now, been demobbed but Bert, under the regulations, had to have his pre-war job back. The Territorial Army was reforming, there were drill halls in a number of places, including a big one in Truro, and his main involvement now was with their control and maintenance. With a jeep at his disposal, he drove all over the county and I often accompanied him in the boneshaker to outlying villages and really got to know Cornwall. I loved the place, it was magical and especially for a girl who had always lived in a town.

Stuart started at the local Methodist primary school, St George's, in the September, at the bottom of the hill, opposite to the fire station.

We lived at the top of the hill, on the corner of Hendra Barton. A barton was a 40-acre field and the road to the side was unadopted. At the end of it, after five houses, was a farm. Our garden was a big, wedge-shaped plot and along a back stone wall covered in rhododendrons ran Lovers' Lane.

At the front, a line of poplars, then the lawn with a round fishpond with its seemingly obligatory water lily and goldfish, which had to be regularly replenished as the seagulls considered them breakfast. From the front gate to the front door, along a long, winding path, there were herbaceous borders on each side, backed by climbing roses on rustic frames, after a lot of hard work by Jimmy. On the right, behind the roses and in front of the rhododendrons, an orchard with apple trees.

Behind the house there was a good-sized kitchen garden with fertile sandy soil, a bed of raspberries, a garden shed and compost area; about half an acre in all.

I was new to gardening and Bert had been just an observer before, except for lawns, which were subject to his military discipline and had to be smooth and weed-free like a bowling green. The lawn mower, powered by Jimmy, was in daily use.

We both learned gardening from books, especially a little one that fitted into my pocket, which became our bible. I still have it, *A Little Encyclopaedia of Gardening*. It is incredibly full of facts, but you needed a magnifying glass or exceptional eyesight to read it.

I planted a row of carrots, according to the book. They came up, nice and green. One day I went out and asked Bert to thin them, handing him the bible. He did just that and then proceeded to replant all the thinnings as the book had not told him what to do with them and he thought it was a pity to waste them. Naturally, they got carrot fly, Bert had not read the next chapter.

Now that we had settled in Cornwall, some of Bert's old friends rediscovered him. We were a cheap holiday destination in 1947 and 1948 but at least they came by car, so I saw parts of the region I wouldn't have otherwise.

Some evenings and most weekends Bert was away exercising with the 'terriers' as the Territorials were known. The drill hall in Truro was quite new and had been marked out with a Badminton Court. I liked the game and played doubles until a couple of weeks before our son Chris was born.

Cornish people were not exactly friendly to foreigners, which included anybody born on the other side of the river Tamar. On Saturday nights, Bert, Stuart and I used to go to the pictures. Afterwards Bert went to the Conservative Club and Stuart and I walked home, usually picking up fish and chips on the way.

Although Bert wasn't Cornish, he had been in a Cornish Regiment since 1917 and his first wife had been a local. When out together we were often stopped by people wanting to talk to him, I was introduced and usually ignored.

One particular occasion sticks in my mind. We were

on the way to the cinema when a couple stopped us. After the introduction, the three-sided conversation continued and finished with the woman saying: 'Do come to tea soon, don't bring the wife.' Did they assume that I spoke and understood no English?

IT must have been about the middle of October 1947, when we were sitting down for tea that Stuart asked: 'Are we going to have a guy to burn and toffee apples?'

'A guy?' I asked, uncomprehendingly, looking at Bert.

'I can't see why not,' he replied. 'I'm certain that I can get some thunderflashes and other bits and pieces. And there is canvas and straw from the van for the bonfire.'

'What's a guy?' I enquired again.

'Oh,' said Stuart, 'Guy Fawkes, you know.'

'I don't know,' I protested.

Bert and Stuart looked at each other. I looked at Bert.

'Why do you burn him?' I asked

'It's a long story,' said Bert. 'In the seventeenth century there was a conspiracy. They were trying to blow up Parliament.'

'Why?' I asked. 'I thought there was always democracy and Parliament here, so why did they try to blow it up?'

'It's very complicated, it was a disagreement between Catholics and the Protestants - anyhow, Guy Fawkes and his friends decided they were going to blow up Parliament when the King was opening it.'

'What do you mean, opening it?' I interjected. 'Was it closed before?'

'No, he was opening it after his coronation for a new session. The conspirators originally wanted to tunnel under the Houses of Parliament but then they found that there were cellars underneath which they could rent, and they were hoarding barrels and barrels of gunpowder there. There were several of them, all Catholics. Guy Fawkes evidently was an expert in munitions so he had the task of setting the thing off. But one of them gave the game away and they were all arrested. Guy Fawkes, a Yorkshireman, was actually found with the fuses in the cellar. He was tortured, as was usual in those days, and sentenced to death.'

'Real, bloody death, hung, drawn and quartered,' added Stuart with relish.

I shuddered.

'And what has that to do with bonfires and toffee apples?' I asked.

'On 5th November, a stuffed dummy, a guy, is put on the bonfire and we celebrate.'

'You celebrate a failed attempt to blow up parliament?'

'Yes and no. When a new King was crowned, people celebrated with a party and bonfires anyway and after the conspirators had been hanged, the guy was added.'

'And drawn and quartered and had their heads displayed on poles.' said Stuart, with almost glee.

'Where do the Poles come in to this? What did they have to do with blowing up Parliament?' I ventured.

'Not that kind of Pole; it's a pole, like a stick.'

'You mean like a perch?'

'No, that's another kind of pole.'

By now I was at sea. My book learning of English history was evidently insufficient.

'Oh, Mum, you are making it all so complicated, it's great fun,' said Stuart. 'We put the guy on a trolly and go around asking for a penny for him and then we have fireworks and toffee apples ...'

'You don't need to go begging to have toffee apples; I can make or buy some,' I said.

'No, it would not be the same; we have to eat them around the fire and the grown-ups can have baked potatoes and soup and beer. The more noise, the better.'

'Sounds to me like a witches Sabbath,' I muttered.

In the end, under Stuart's instruction, I used sacking and straw to make a guy. He was huge, Stuart thought that nobody would have one as big. Some of his friends nailed together a wooden platform and some old pram wheels, the guy was tied to it and wheeled down the hill into Truro proper.

More straw and wood was used to build a big bonfire on the vegetable patch in the garden and the guy was enthroned. Bert acquired some fireworks and stuffed them into the bonfire which turned out to be not such a good idea.

As I had given up sugar in tea or coffee so as to be able to make jam, that was used for the toffee apples and baking potatoes under the bonfire was not difficult for Bert who was so used to army ways. It was the biggest bonfire in the neighbourhood, Stuart got his friends round and some of their parents, as well as the neighbours. They all thought that, for a foreigner, I had done really well.

THE only friends I made in Truro were the pharmacist and his wife, who were equally ostracised for not being locals. Our friendship started when I went there and asked to buy a large bottle of olive oil and one of arachid (groundnut) oil to use in cooking.

The restricted amount of butter, margarine and lard - something I had not seen before - available was insufficient for baking and Bert liked his cakes. I thought that if I used oil in ordinary cooking, that would leave enough over for the rest.

People normally bought olive oil in tiny bottles to warm by the spoonful and pour into aching ears, whilst arachid oil was used to make emulsions by the chemist. When I asked him for large bottles of the stuff, he called his wife and before long we were in a heated discussion on the use of oils in the household.

He managed to get me them and, subsequently, Bert's favourite jam tarts and lardy cakes were never absent from the tea table. As a foursome we often went to the pictures and to the dances at the drill hall. I loved to dance, Bert didn't.

I'd get the first and the last dance with him, both obligatory and for the rest of the time he propped up the bar remembering, at times, to send a young subaltern down to ask me to dance. He would have preferred to do so with his girlfriend but an order was an order.

Bert's idea of dance was to march along the room and turn at the corners, more or less in time with the music and often stepping on my toes. It was infuriating. It had become usual during the war years for ladies to dance together but it was not a custom I was used to and I didn't like it.

WHEN we visited Bristol things were different. Will loved old time dancing even though Doll didn't. Renee, their eldest daughter and Albert, her fiancée were also great fans so I had plenty of opportunities. I was introduced to the Dashing White Sergeant, the Progressive Barn Dance, the Military Two-step, the Gay Gordon's, the Valetta and many other dances; all great fun.

For our first Christmas, we came up to Bristol to spend it with the family. On Christmas Eve, everyone congregated at the British Legion Club at Staple Hill. Christmas morning, all the men met up at the one in Redland, above the Victoria Rooms, before going to their own homes for the formal dinner. Not yet turkey or goose, it was either chicken or pork, and then to listen to the King's Christmas message. Boxing Day saw everybody assembled at Harry and Elaine's because they had the largest sitting room. After tea and washing up, the female members of the family settled around the fire and the men, all seven of them, remained around the dining table, setting the world to rights. As sometimes happens, we ladies stopped talking and turned towards the men. We looked at each other and burst out laughing. They were all talking at the same time and no-one was listening. A common occurrence for the Knills.

THE food rationing in Britain was nothing in comparison to what it had been in Czechoslovakia, I found the allowances here were generous. There were also new things to get acquainted with such as Branston Pickle, the most popular accompaniment to cheese in sandwiches. It is an acquired taste and I did not take to it any more than I liked salad cream, ketchup, HP and Worcester sauces. I felt that all they did was hide the actual taste of the food and I have not really changed my mind on that. I also struggled with those essentials, tea and coffee.

Tea, of the type favoured by Doll, was in the form of PG Tips which, to me, seemed like dust. Back home, we used leaf and, although more expensive, when I bought the Ceylon variety I was used to, it went much further. I became, albeit reluctantly, familiar with what was then considered coffee in Britain, Camp Coffee with hot milk. In Cornwall, I found that I could buy green coffee beans which were not on ration and roast them in a frying pan kept especially for that purpose. I bought a coffee pot, an electric one, which had a tap at the bottom, like on a samovar, and was back in coffee heaven.

Milk was brought to our door by a land girl. She came

on a horse drawn cart, which had rubber wheels, with churns on the waggon. You went out with a white enamel mini churn which had a lid chained to its handle and the appropriate amount of milk was decanted into it. I had no idea whether or not it was pasteurised and I always boiled the milk before use, just to be on the safe side. I didn't drink milk as it did not agree with me but the land girl told me how to make clotted cream from it, perfect with my scones.

Sugar was rationed and the jam in the shops was not particularly nice. We had a big garden with apple trees and rather neglected raspberry bushes and a strawberry bed, so it seemed obvious that I should make some. As a result, I gave up taking sugar in my tea so I could produce enough jam to have a fresh pot each week. I also tried to dry apples, as we had when I grew up, but here the slices, suspended on knotted string, just rotted in the damp atmosphere.

MY periods had stopped while I was in the camps, which is a normal occurrence for women if they are undernourished and traumatised. After the war, they were irregular and remained so. We took no precautions as both of us assumed that I would be unable to conceive, so when I started to be sick in the mornings in the autumn of 1947 I attributed it to my temperamental stomach reacting to unfamiliar English food.

Since Bert was an officer in the regular army, a local doctor had been designated to care for family members as the NHS did not yet exist. Eventually I made an appointment and, yes, I was pregnant. Bert was pleased, mother ecstatic and I was somewhat bemused as I had not expected it, but came to accept it.

I started buying Winceyette to make nightgowns, then nappies, both terry and soft lining. Then mother sent over a baby carriage of woven willows and lacquered white, something not seen in the UK before. A cot was bought, I made and embroidered quilts for it and old sheets, soft from lots of washing, were cut down to fit.

The smallest bedroom, looking out over the back garden and orchard, was painted white and the floor covered in lino, everything was made ready.

Following a visit by the midwife, one other item had to be prepared; a maternity pack, which I had to take with me to the maternity home, when the baby was due. It contained everything that was needed for the birth and immediately after, both for mother and addition. The assumption was that nothing material would be provided by them, what I did not take I would have to do without, it was a long list.

In those days it was considered unimaginable that a woman would not have a female friend with her when it came to giving birth. That presented me with a problem. Of Bert's family, Doll was the one I knew best but she had to look after her two girls and her husband. It would, therefore, have been impossible to ask and, in any case, I did not feel that close to her. Similarly, neither Connie nor Elaine had children but I would not have considered either of them as suitable.

Mother was unable to travel over from Bratislava being fully occupied with re-establishing the family business, looking after Tomy, my brother and Magda, her niece, whose parents had perished in the Holocaust.

But two of her cousins now lived in England, Edith and Gertie. Edith, being ten years older than me had been more mother's friend than mine and had always been considered a very capable person. She had been a solicitor's clerk. Gertie was my age, but had always been overshadowed and, to a certain extent, overruled by Edith.

The Woman with Nine Lives

They had both managed to escape from Czechoslovakia to Palestine on the ship *Exodus*. Their two brothers, Bela and Karl, had preceded them there by some means or other, which was never talked about.

Edith had married Eric Fisher, an architect, while he was serving with the British Expeditionary Force there. Gertie married Kelley, an Irishman, who had also been in the forces and who worked in oil exploration in the Middle East. Edith and I had maintained contact and she was living in Reading. Gertie and her husband were somewhere abroad but his contract was due to expire and they were expected to come to England or, perhaps, go to Ireland where Kelley's mother still lived.

Unfortunately, due to my erratic menstrual cycle, it was not possible to establish the exact date when the baby was due. The doctor and I made an inspired guess and fixed the end of March as a likely date of birth. I wrote to Edith asking whether she would be willing to be 'mother' to me, to come down to Cornwall, stay with us until the baby was born and see me through the first week or so afterwards. She agreed to, Eric could spare her for three weeks and it would be good for her to come over.

And then we waited. And waited. The end of March came and went. When, by the end of the first week in April, there was still no sign of a baby wanting to be born I arranged to see the doctor. On examining me he shook his head and said: 'I can't imagine how this could have happened, the child is in the breach position. You should just wait until the pains start and then go quickly to the infirmary. It would be a good idea for your husband to go with you, we might have to do a Caesarean section.' I had no idea what he meant.

So back home I went and continued waiting. It was not until the 15th that my pains started.

Bert said: 'I can't possibly go with you. We are opening a new drill hall and Emanuel Shinwell, the Minister for Defence, is coming, I have to be there. Edith will have to stay at home because Stuart can't be left on his own. You'll just have to manage.' Army always came first.

Off I went with my maternity pack to Truro Infirmary where I was rushed into a single room then along a corridor, away from the main female ward, not feeling at all well and in considerable pain. The rest was rather a haze of anaesthetics, being told that I had a healthy baby boy and continually asked where my husband was. When I told them that he was at the opening of a new drill hall, there was consternation.

When, next day, Bert came to have a look at his new son, Matron forbad him entry. 'You could not be there for your wife when it was a matter of life and death, so you can wait a few days before seeing your son,' she told him. Matrons were a law unto themselves in those days and Bert was not allowed to see his Chris for almost a week.

EDITH had been staying with us for the allotted three weeks and now Eric was anxious for her to come back. So she got in touch with Gertie who was somewhere in the wilds of Ireland while Kelley looked for another job and asked if she and her little girl would like to come and stay with me for a bit.

Bert and I talked it over and, although her little girl would be the first such that Bert had encountered, we agreed that it would be a good idea for her to come and keep me company. On the day of their arrival two cabs drew up one full of suitcases, the other with Kelley, Gert, and their little daughter.

Kelley said; 'You didn't think I would let Gertie come without checking up it's the right place.' But in actual fact he too had come to stay and became an embarrassment. Bert, with his usual goodwill, took him to the Conservative Club and to the officers' mess and found out months later that Kelley had borrowed money from practically everyone, saying Bert would repay them.

Unfortunately, there were problems for me and the baby. Chris refused to breastfeed and I developed mastitis. Win had died of breast cancer so you can imagine that Bert was rather apprehensive, while not saying a lot.

The NHS had only just started and Bert didn't trust the local doctor because he was the one who hadn't treated Win properly or in time. It was, therefore, decided that Stuart, Chris and I would go to Bristol and Kelly and Gertie were told they had to leave.

They departed in two taxis in the morning and we caught the train in the afternoon.

They didn't actually leave Truro but billeted themselves on my neighbours, saying we had thrown them out. That explained why our neighbours were off-hand with us when we eventually got back.

The Bristol medics sorted out my problems and Chris flourished from that moment onwards. Bert, who had taken compassionate leave, found on our return to Truro that some of the battalions had been amalgamated, his post had disappeared and he was now attached to the West African Rifles.

In June, when Chris was five months old, Bert departed to Nigeria with his uniforms made in Bond Street and I was left to cope as best as I could with Stuart and the baby in Truro.

BACK in July 1947, a letter arrived one morning from Customs and Excise to tell us that a sealed container had arrived from Czechoslovakia and it had to be opened in front of the officials who would decide what part, if any, could be allowed into the country duty-free.

A copy of the manifest was enclosed and we were asked to contact them to arrange a suitable date for its delivery and inspection.

It appeared to be the size of a small railway carriage and the only place to put it would be backed up the drive so as not to interfere with the neighbours. The manifest was full of surprises. I knew that mother was sending me the family silver as well as the Karlsbad china, which was her wedding present and all the other wedding gifts which were mainly crystal, china and pottery.

There were also feather-beds and pillows filled with Hungarian goose down, so much linen that 60 years later I still use some. Towels and tea towels, pots and pans, some old Persian carpets, a beautiful bedroom suite in Canadian birds' eye maple and boxes full of fabrics for clothes; linen, cotton, wool, silk.

A sewing machine, two armchairs and a round table, boxes of piano music, folders with embroidery and knitting patterns and files of photographs. I had brought two big suitcases with me when I first came to England four months before but here there were boxes of furs and winter clothes, silk underwear by the dozen, enough table linen for the most magnificent household and every item embroidered with my initials.

Since I was officially classed as 'an officer's wife returning from abroad' I could bring my personal possessions and also antiques, which meant that the silver and the carpets were no problem, but duty may have to be paid on anything that was brand new. We came to an arrangement with Customs that duty would be paid only on the fabrics.

A couple of days later a joiner came to install our new bedroom suite. There was no way it could go up the staircase with its two bends, so the window had to be taken out and a pulley installed.

The furniture which had been in Bert and Win's bedroom we sent to Frank, Bert's brother, who, also with his wife Connie's father, had just moved to a big house in Bower Ashton, near Bristol. Needless to say, every time we moved we had the same problem with the bedroom suite, windows had to come out. After Bert died and I moved to Grange Cottage in Leeds, I dismantled and disposed of it, except for a small dressing table which is still in my studio.

The container itself proved very useful beside the house as there was no garage. It became the place for bikes and storage and was eventually dismantled and re-erected outside the back door as a washhouse.

A corrugated roof covered the paving between the back door and the washhouse, washing lines were strung up so that wet washing did not have to be dried all over the house, drainage was put in and the washing machine – a wedding present from uncle Bela – was installed.

It was a rather primitive affair that had to be filled via a hose with cold water, there was a big paddle to move the washing around and on top was a hand-operated wringer, which had the unfortunate habit of ripping off buttons from shirts, unless you folded them carefully to be on the inside. Tension had to be adjusted by a screw on top and a pair of wooden grips enabled you to lift the, inevitably boiled, washing to the wringer.

This new contraption did not, however, obviate the need for a wooden trough and a washboard and stiff brush, which were needed to remove stains as washing powders then, made up of soda and soap shavings, were not really effective.

Rinsing had to be done in the wooden trough and washday Mondays were hard work, especially after Chris was born and nappies had to be soaked, washed, rinsed and dried.

The corrugated cover on the walkway proved really useful as, in wet weather, Chris in his pram could still stay out in the fresh, albeit damp, air.

Unfortunately, the problems with my left shoulder and neck, the result of a car smash on the way to the Czech mission at Bad Oyenhausen restarted. I could not turn my head to the left and had difficulty lifting Chris. The doctor advised a series of shortwave treatment and massage.

Every day I pushed the pram up Pidar Street to the Infirmary for the sessions. By Friday each week my neck and shoulder were decidedly better but come Monday we were back to square one. After six weeks I gave up, painkillers would have to do. Nightmares of the past also persisted and nightly administration of barbiturates was not really the answer.

My only release was music. The piano had been tuned, my music had arrived in the container but hammering the keyboard, although giving me relief, woke up Chris and it was not easy to get him back to sleep.

Once a fortnight I took the train to Bodmin with Chris and Stuart, so that Stuart could meet his maternal grandmother. She told me lots about the family history, most of which was confidential, and I still respect that she had the courage and compassion to talk to me freely.

Except for Win's pearls, which I eventually gave to Stuart for his wife Barbara, I gave her all of Win's jewellery, which Bert had bestowed upon me. I felt that it belonged more to her.

THE summer turned to autumn and as rain and storms battered the house, walking became well-nigh impossible. I felt more and more alone. Bert wrote every second day but the letters came in batches, often a week went by without my hearing from him.

I took lots of photos of Chris and sent them in my letters with appropriate captions, so he could see the progress of his youngest son. I also encouraged Stuart to write but had hardly any contact with Bert's family in Bristol. Edith kept in touch, but was busy with her own first child, Francis.

On 5th November I got a telegram from Bert reading, 'Happy Birthday – happy returns of the day'. Somehow he had mixed up Guy Fawkes day with my birthday on the 25th November. Couldn't he even remember that? Something snapped.

I had been taking the local paper, trying to find out what made the Cornish tick and found that the local MP was scheduled to have a surgery the next week. I pushed the pram there and asked to speak to him. He was one of the Foot family. The pram stayed outside and hardly had I started to explain my situation when Chris started to cry, loudly.

The MP asked: 'Does he cry a lot?'

'Yes, he does,' I said. 'He is not a contented baby and I am often at my wit's end. Plus there is my stepson, aged nine, and it is getting impossible for me to cope,' I told him.

'Where is your family?'

'In Czechoslovakia, in Bratislava. Now that it is a communist country it is impossible for mother to come. Also she has my younger brother and her niece to look after. She has to work for them as they are still studying.'

'What about your husband's family?' He queried.

I said, resignedly, 'All of them live in Bristol and have

their own young families to look after. I have nobody to call on to help and when I am not well I just have to keep going somehow. I do wish my husband was back in the UK.'

The MP asked, 'Where is he stationed?'

'He is with the West African Rifles in Nigeria,' I advised.

'Could you not join him?'

'No, that is not possible with a child under one and we would also have to place Stuart in a boarding school as there are no educational facilities there for him and he has been through too much already for that.' I then explained what had happened to Win.

The MP considered for a moment and said: 'They really should not have posted him so far away.'

'He is a soldier and has been one all his life,' I replied. 'He obeys orders. Bert would not have thought of doing anything else.'

'Well, we'll just have to see what I can do,' he said trying to be reassuring.

He was as good as his word. Two weeks before Christmas Bert was flown back to the UK on compassionate grounds. He was amazed. He had never heard of something like that happening before. His chests and cases came by boat and arrived in the spring.

I don't know whether he was pleased or not, he liked Africa and the Africans. He brought one thing back though, which he had not intended. He forgot that he was supposed to continue taking anti-malarial medication for some weeks after leaving Africa and he went down with Tertial Malaria and Blackwater Fever.

WE spent that Christmas with his brother Frank and Connie in Bower Ashton, with Bert so ill that we wondered whether he would survive. Frank and the brothers often went to the British Legion Club. One morning he told me that he had met a couple of Czechs there who really wanted to talk to me and said they would be coming that afternoon.

They duly arrived and asked whether they could talk to me in confidence. We went into the drawing room, which was unheated, and I asked them why they wanted to speak to me, since I did not know them.

They said that they were employed by the Czech Government and as I was married to an officer, they expected he would give me news about army matters and that I could tell these to them. I explained that it was not something that I could do.

First of all, I did not think Bert would have the kind of information they wanted and, even if he did, he would hardly be likely to tell me. Secondly, if he had, I wouldn't betray his confidence.

They said that if I did not comply it would be bad for my family in Bratislava and with that they left. I was very worried and told Bert what had happened. He told me not to worry, he would get it sorted.

I never heard from the two men again and have no idea what happened.

Letters to and from Czechoslovakia were now being censored by the authorities there, so mother and I were very careful about what we put into our thin blue airmail exchanges.

Bert was very ill for several months. As the fits of malaria decreased, he got psoriasis and lost all his hair. It re-grew without any sign of grey, returning his fetching blond locks.

1949

IT must have been about February. Bert was still on sick leave, recuperating and waiting to get his next posting. I was still finding solace, or relative peace, in music.

The piano was in the drawing room and in the dining room next door Bert was playing with Chris on the floor. The doors were open.

Suddenly I heard Bert shout: 'Don't stop playing but just look.'

I did, and tottering towards me was ten-month-old Chris, beaming all over his face, just like his father, drawn towards me by the music. 'Muskick,' he said.

We were getting worried about where Bert would be sent next. There was no vacancy for him in the DCLI. British troops were being withdrawn from India and they brought their families with them. A huge hotel in Droitwich was requisitioned and became a married families' camp. Bert was posted there as second-in-command.

Droitwich was a long way from Truro and since there was now no reason for us to stay there, we started to think of moving. We had no idea how long the posting would be for or the length of time it would take the army to rehouse all these families, but we thought that it would make sense to relocate to Bristol, to be nearer to Bert's extended family.

For the time being, though, I had to stay in Truro.

Our black Ford car. Father, mother, cousin Gerti, Iby and Tomy.

Life Two

*

I had not seen mother or Tomy for ages. Mother had by now re-married to uncle Imre, father's cousin, who was no stranger to me. He had survived Auschwitz too but their respective spouses had not.

1950

UNCLE IMRE, as I continued to call him, had two daughters, Lizzie and Ibi, my namesake. Ibi was a couple of years older than me and she had come with the second transport from Auschwitz to Lippstadt. She contracted typhoid and was one of those I had nursed. She had met an American soldier, married him and eventually they went to live in Israel. They had both been guests at my wedding.

My brother Tomy was now at university studying engineering. Niece Magda wanted to study architecture but finished up as a hospital almoner. Czechoslovakia was now a communist country. Mother had not seen her first grandchild, nor me for years so Bert suggested that Stuart should go up to Droitwich with him and to school there while I paid an extended visit to Bratislava.

Travel abroad was not easy at this time. I had to get Chris on to my passport and permission from the Home Office to travel to Czechoslovakia, as I had been through positive clearing in respect of the Official Secrets Act, and signed the appropriate papers in Germany. I also had to get a visa.

Eventually the official business was completed. Chris and I were on a flight to Prague and then, in a ramshackle Dakota, on to Bratislava. At the front and back of the plane were fully armed soldiers and the order was that we had to keep our seatbelts on at all times and not move. Hijacking, even back then, appeared to be a danger they feared.

To keep a less than two-year-old, lively boy still and in one place for over an hour was just not possible. Chris wiggled out of his seatbelt, crawled and staggered to the soldiers at the front and thought that their guns were his toys. When the soldiers, laughing, refused to hand them over, he tottered over to the back of the plane and tried to do the same with those at there.

It was hilarious but most of the passengers sat stony-faced, looking straight ahead. This kind of humour was not usual under this new regime where people barely dared to look over their shoulders.

Mother's business, the family one, had not yet been nationalised and uncle Imre still had the pharmacy 'Der rote Krebs' (the red lobster), situated by the old town gate, so much of their time they were at work. His chemist shop, which had been in existence since the Middle Ages, eventually became the Museum of Pharmacy.

A big woman, Maria, from the country, was now cook

and maid. Mother had acquired a pushchair for Chris as well as a fur coat and muff for me as the weather in January was really cold, but bright and sunny.

We went for long walks, I re-acquainting myself with the town and rediscovering the few of my contemporaries who had survived and stayed. Newspapers were controlled and only gave out local news and those stories deemed suitable for general consumption by the communist authorities. They had to adhere strictly to party lines.

There was nothing about England in them and I wanted to keep up with what was happening there. I had had to register us with the police and also, for security reasons, with the British consulate, just down the road from where we lived. They told me that there was a reading room at the British Council where I could scan the newspapers and borrow books.

I went there. I had felt like a stranger in Cornwall and now one here and worried that I had done the wrong thing by going to live in England.

I had not realised either that I was being followed wherever I went. One day, I had gone on my own to a department store to do some shopping, leaving Chris with Maria, who adored him. Having got my purchases, I left the store by an alternative exit which led onto a different street. I got home and was sitting in the living room, when the doorbell went. A couple of minutes later Maria came in, holding a little man in a leather coat by the collar and shouting at him.

'She is here, can't you see? Where else would she be?'

The little man was struggling, being lifted nearly off his feet and shaken by Maria as if he was a rag doll. It seemed that my shadow had lost me, panicked and come to find out where I was. He apologised profoundly, he felt very uncomfortable, especially as Maria was still holding and shaking him, but explained that his life would not be worth living if he had lost sight of me.

I told him that wherever I went I would come back here. He said that was not what was worrying him, he needed to know who I met and talked to. That was the deciding factor for me. I could not face living in such a country and arranged to go back to England, to Bert, and try to make there my home. I returned in March 1950.

WE decided to move to Bristol but it took us some time to find a house we liked. We eventually moved in to 28 Eagle Road. The determining factor was that it had a fishpond in the garden. Not just a small round one with water lilies, like the one in Truro, but a big rectangular one, with a deep part in the middle and low shelving on three sides.

It was ideal, according to Bert: 'We'll breed our own goldfish here,' he said.

The married families' camp in Droitwich, which had extensive grounds, also included a huge pond, as large as a swimming pool, but all his efforts to keep fish were completely unsuccessful, no doubt due to the number of children using it as a paddling pool. Errant seagulls constantly hovering over it were probably a contributory factor to the disappearance of the goldfish there too.

The BBC transmitter was at this time not far from Droitwich. Its workings were cooled with water which, in turn, was discharged into large outdoor tanks to cool down. Whatever the air temperature, they were always lukewarm and proved to be an ideal environment for goldfish of all kinds.

Somehow, probably through their shared love of cricket and attendance at the Worcestershire CCC members' pavilion, one of the engineers and Bert became friends.

I used to come up to Droitwich whenever possible and can remember, on one occasion, going to the transmission station and seeing these tanks. We took a loaf of bread with us and Bert's friend took a bunch of keys out of his pocket and rattled them against the railings. The water appeared to boil and dozens of goldfish and koi carp, all of them enormous, of every possible shade and variety - gold and white, spotted, striped or flecked, ones with long tails, others short, some even with two tails - streamed towards us and threshed the water in front of us with mouths open.

The loaf was broken up, thrown in and the pieces often caught mid-air by ravenous, fighting fish. Some of their descendants came to stock our pond in Eagle Road, arriving in a container converted from an empty petrol can. They liked their new environment, especially after we stretched netting across the pond to deter seagulls and any visiting cats.

When they started to breed, Bert lowered the water level and the small fry slipped across the wall into the shallow area where they were safe from the big fish which would have had them for breakfast. They were assiduously fed with dried and fresh fish food and enjoyed themselves and gave joy to us as we saw them growing.

Our garage was at the bottom of the garden and was approached by a lane from the end of the road. On the other side of the lane was a tall brick wall. It was not until we had moved in that we realised that it hid an embankment at the bottom along which ran the mainline train from Bristol to London. At this time, the trains did not run so frequently and, unless the driver blew the whistle, we were scarcely aware of their passing.

The back garden was quite big but nowhere near as large as the one in Truro. From the French doors of the dining room there was a paved area, then the lawn. Next to the large fishpond was an area of crazy paving and then, what could or should have been a kitchen garden.

On the left, a path led from the side of the house and the kitchen door the whole length of the garden to the garage. On the left of the path was a wide herbaceous border. Bert's knowledge of gardening was still limited but straight lines were his forte. Our lawns were always the envy of the neighbourhood as not a single weed was allowed to take root in it.

The lawnmower, an ancient pre-war model, was in nearly daily use and woe betide anybody who dared to disturb the even stripes of the green. The grass was for looking at, not for walking on.

The herbaceous border was a different matter and remained my territory, as did the kitchen garden. Admittedly, my expertise was hardly more extensive then Bert's, but I did read up on it. The Bristol Flower Show on the Downs was a place of pleasure and discovery for me and enlarged the rudimentary knowledge I had acquired in Truro.

The Nash's next door were keen gardeners too, they even had a small greenhouse. It was entirely dedicated to Norman's hobby of chrysanthemums. I had never seen mopheads in white and yellow as big as the ones he produced and exhibited at the local show.

The points of a pair of eyebrow tweezers were coated in fine cotton-wool and he spent hours getting every petal aligned in perfect harmony. That he eventually showed his chrysanthemums at the Bristol Show was the apotheosis of his efforts.

It was there that I saw dahlias for the first time, in magnificent profusion. They captivated me. It was not the big showy ones that I found entrancing, but the pompoms so I ordered a dozen tubers. They were deep scarlet with white tips and I planted them along the long border. Leaves appeared in due course and then a straight stem with quite a heavy bud at the top.

That weekend Bert was on leave from Droitwich and announced that he would do some gardening. I thought it would give me the opportunity to go into town without Chris in the pushchair and left him in the playpen in the garden with Bert.

When I got back, Bert was keen to show me all he had done. The front garden was an exceedingly trim lawn bordered by narrow beds of hardy annuals in full bloom and a path leading to the heavy oak front door, from which I had stripped the paint and which shone from the coats of oil which had been lovingly rubbed into it; it looked idyllic.

But what Bert wanted me really to see was the back garden. So I was led through the French doors to admire the pristine striped lawn and the weeded crazy paving but when looking towards the long border, in which the dahlias had stood proudly with their single bud about to open, I saw instead twelve straight stalks.

'My dahlias! What has happened to the dahlias?' I gasped.

'Dahlias?' questioned Bert. 'There were some knobs there, I thought it would look better if they were cut off; they made the garden look untidy.'

I was flabbergasted. My prize dahlias had been beheaded. It took weeks for them to recover from the brutality but oddly enough, to me at least, such drastic treatment must have been what they needed because, instead of just one stem, several sprang up and rather than a single bloom, there was a profusion of flowers that became the envy of the neighbourhood.

I REMEMBER being shown the original indenture of Thomas Knill being accepted as a brightsmith in the City of Bristol.

The apprenticeship was to last for seven years, after which he would be admitted to the Guild of Brightsmiths, which would entitle him to become a Freeman of the city. Thomas was probably twelve years old at the time and the document stated that his father had died. I have a photo of him.

Tom, Bert's younger brother, showed me the document. It had been passed on to him, as he bore the same name as his grandfather. Tom also had, apparently, Bert's gold medal which he had been awarded for winning a marathon in Darjeeling and which he had given to his mother. The house in which Bert's parents had lived in the St Paul district of Bristol had been bombed.

Thomas Knill's brother, William, went to London and, according to family legend, became Lord Mayor, was knighted and as a result, the baronetcy of Knill was restored, the male line having died out some time before.

Knill Court near the village of Knill was burned down during the Second World War – a girls' boarding school had been evacuated there – and the ruins were deemed to be haunted, so I was told when I visited the site in the 1960's.

The old church was there and still in use, with the shields and coat of arms of the Knills, who were still being buried in the graveyard, evident. The ruins had been offered to the National Trust, they overlooked Offa's Dyke and the Knills were one of the Lords of the Marches but the Trust were not prepared to pay for it and declined the offer.

A local farmer took over the land, took out salvaged wooden carvings and nailed them up in his farmhouse, put concrete partitions into the original tithe barn but had to incorporate the one remaining archway in a building. Several large houses were built on the land.

BERT was one of seven children, five boys and two girls but one of them, May, died in childhood. That left, in order of birth: Alfred, Doll, Bert, Frank, Tom and Harry. Harry was the only one who went to grammar school, the older brothers contributed to the fees, yet he was the one who did least with his life.

We all got together at Christmas and there was a tradition on Christmas Eve that they all went to the British Legion Club in Redland where there was a big raffle, then on Christmas Day, Bert phoned them all up, in turn.

Bert had presented me with a copy of Mrs. Beeton's classic cookery book and, having collected copious dried fruit despite rationing, I decided to make a Christmas cake for the family. The Cook Sergeant had the same idea for the Major at Droitwich Spa and gave Bert a foot square slice and Doll, not believing that I would know a traditional recipe, also made one for us. Then, at the raffle at the club, I won another and I don't even like it.

The Knills were all keen on sport, especially cricket. They claimed, proudly, that they could put out a full team, including umpires and often did.

They played at the Westbury-on-Trym grounds. Wives were deputed to provide and serve the tea, which was seen as an integral part of the family effort. The only available position for me, once I had been initiated into cricket lore, was to be scorer, deemed a very responsible job indeed.

Tom and his wife Elsie lived near to the Gloucestershire cricket ground so, in summer, once Chris was in a pushchair, I would take him there on the bus to the match. That was the only acceptable excuse for there not being a hot dinner on the table. Bert would pick us up after work from Tom's and take us home.

While we lived in Bristol, mother came to visit. We took her to the Military Tattoo in Bath, which impressed her enormously and then, one afternoon, to the cricket. It was a sunny day and she opened her sunshade to the consternation of people sitting behind us in the stand.

I could not get her to understand the very particular ins and outs of cricket. It had confused her enough when, at my wedding, the padre had made numerous references in cricketing terms. Mother saw it as just another of those outlandish English customs.

In Eagle Road our life settled into a routine and I was accepted from the word go. It was a nice feeling. Civil Defence and amateur dramatics at the church hall occupied my evenings. On Saturday, in the winter, the men went to support Bristol City. They always finished up at Frank's place in Bower Ashton. On Sunday afternoons Harry and Elaine came over to us to have tea and we played canasta before they took the bus back to Redlands.

OUR move to Bristol was also actually rather fortuitous as Stuart was changing from primary to secondary school. He had been a chorister at Kenwyn Church in Truro, so we thought it would be nice if he could go as one to Bristol Cathedral School.

He went to the audition but unfortunately his voice had started to break early and he couldn't reach the high notes anymore. But Bristol Cathedral School seemed the right place, so he entered as a paying scholar.

Somehow or other, he and the school did not live in harmony together and towards the end of the academic year the headmaster asked to see Bert and I, and we were tactfully told to find him somewhere else to study. They recommend St Mary Redclyff and it suited him down to the ground, he finished up as head boy.

Chris loved his little pedal car and with the garden being quite long and the side gate locked, he used to go up and down to his heart's content.

One day the dustbin men left the side gate open and we couldn't find Chris. In Keynsham nearby, there was a high security prison and the previous day a child murderer had escaped and people had been warned to keep their offspring indoors.

Needless to say we panicked and all the neighbourhood started to look for Chris in his little blue pedal car, including the police. He was found, pedalling along the road towards Temple Meads station and giving appropriate hand signals. He said he had gone to meet his father as he came home from Droitwich.

Eventually Bert was stationed in Bristol, with the Gloucester's TA battalion. It was considered right for Chris, now three, to go to a prep school and there was one in Redlands, not far from the TA head office where, to my amazement at that young age, they taught him to write.

Harry and Elaine lived in that area, so Bert took Chris up to school every morning, fetched him at lunchtime when they went to Elaine's to eat, and then she met him after school and Bert eventually picked him up and brought him home.

There was one memorable New Year's Eve Ball that the Terriers held in the Victoria Rooms in Bristol where Chris, in a miniature uniform, was stationed at the top of the balcony to greet the New Year in, while Bert, in a sheet and holding a sickle, was walking around downstairs signifying the old one going out.

I NOW had free time on my hands and thought it would be rather nice to have a job. I applied as a personal assistant at a nearby factory and got an interview but must have terrified the boss with my knowledge of languages.

I also wanted something to occupy my mind in the evening because Bert frequently had to be at the Terriers as part of his role.

The nearby church had an amateur theatrical society and I joined it with enthusiasm although, with my accent, I ended up just doing scenery, except at Christmas. It was Frank's idea that I should join the Civil Defence which, as an ex-army man, he was in.

There were certain age restrictions and, because I was young, I could only join the ambulance section – rescue being for males only – and gained my Red Cross first aid and eventually my advanced certificate. Since I had learned bandaging in the detention centre in Hungary, my party piece was treating a head wound, for which you needed two bandages.

Frank's business as a tailor wasn't doing very well because of restrictions on material for new clothes, coupons were still in use, so he thought it would be nice for him and Bert to have a business together and that I could work in. They bought a tobacconist and sweet shop, next door to a grocer's shop on the outskirts of Bristol.

With Bert at work and Frank only there occasionally, it fell to me although I wasn't paid. But it worked out to be a lifesaver for Doll's daughter, Renee, who was engaged. Their wedding was postponed again and again because they couldn't find anywhere to live so she and Albert took over the flat above the shop.

Keeping a shop was boring, especially as we only had

sweets and tobacco to sell, so before long I introduced fruit and veg the grocer didn't sell and it made life a little bit more interesting. Eventually Renee and Albert managed to find a house and Frank and Bert decided to sell the shop.

Since Bert was due to retire from the army, he and Frank were getting more ambitious looking for alternative investments.

The Woman with Nine Lives

Life Three

*

D ownend was a thriving, up and coming suburb. Bert's idea of having a pub and Frank's of owning a fish and chip shop there did not meet with approval on my part.

By the end of 1954, the pair thought that they had found absolutely the right property cum shop. I had just found out I was pregnant again, not something I had anticipated under any circumstances.

With Frank unaware and then horrified when he subsequently discovered, the decision was taken to buy the property and we sold Eagle Road very quickly. I couldn't see any problems. We moved in March 1955 and Pauline was born four months later. On this occasion Bert stayed on the right side of the nurses and got me to hospital before, going shooting on the ranges with the Terriers.

Bert's farewell from the organisation was a memorable occasion. I vividly remember him staggering the length of the function room, carefully holding his pint of beer and making sure it didn't spill over. There were no laws about drinking and driving, but I was getting worried about his insistence on taking me home that evening, so I got one of the terriers to puncture the tyres on the car. When he went to inspect them he gently keeled over. His language was exceptionally vivid. We took a taxi.

PAULINE was born on 9th July 1955 at Southmead Maternity Hospital. She, just like Chris, came out weeks later than expected. However, unlike her brother, she was a happy contented baby, and everybody adored her.

While I was at Southmead, and in those days you stayed in for at least ten days, our household was enlarged when Bert acquired a dog.

He had gone to visit a friend of his, who was a vet. While talking to him a policeman came in with a dog and asked for him to be put down. He had been posted to London and the mutt, a trained police one, would not tolerate another master.

While the conversation was going on, the dog called Joe rose, walked over to Bert and put his head on his knee and that was that. Bert had been accepted. Joe decided that his task was to guard Pauline. Her pram was put out at the side of the house and he lay down beside it and nobody was allowed to get near. He would only accept food from Bert, the dog became a treasured part of the household.

At the front of the house was a footpath with a wide grass verge which Joe loved to walk on. Traffic on the road could be quite heavy. One day he stepped off the verge onto the road and a lorry hit him and killed him outright. It took a long time before we got another dog.

NUMBER 73 Badminton Road, Downend, was a typical old fashioned grocer's shop with brown wooden shelves. In front of the counter were biscuit tins with glass lids and there was a cold room built-in from the kitchen. Bacon was delivered by the side and I had to learn how to bone it, cut off the gammon, middle and belly pork.

I knew nothing about groceries, but there was a Grocers Association in Bristol and I went to classes to learn the difference between the varieties of sultanas and currants and the like. Cheese was always cheddar and came as a truckle and had coarse linen on it and we used a slicer to cut it into chunks. We decided we would also have greengrocery and at five o'clock in the morning I had to go to market.

All the proceeds from the sale of Eagle Road went into the business because Frank had no money, although he and Bert were partners and he got half of the profits. Doll used to help in the shop and she got paid and all her groceries at cost price and we also had another helper, Mrs. Wickes.

Chris was now going to Downend Primary school and though Pauline went to a childminder and then nursery school, she used to be under our feet in the shop and fed biscuits by Bert.

In those days people put in a grocery order and Bert bought an A30 so he and Frank could deliver them in turn.

We made the acquaintance of Dr. Audrey Fox, our GP. Her husband was an engineer at Filton and Audrey and I became friends. They were planning the construction of the M4 and the Ministry of Transport was buying up land and was willing to let out parcels of it on short term leases.

Mink had become a fashionable fur and Bert thought it would be a marvellous idea to have a mink farm.

On the land next to the Fox's garden we rented a section and a structure was put up for albino mink. The cages had wire bottoms with a tray underneath to catch all the dirt. When one of the females came on heat the male's cage was put on top and she could not escape his amorous advances. Feeding the mink was an issue. It became my job to prepare their food and the garage floor was emptied for that purpose. We used to get a complete tripe once a week from which all vestiges of fat had to be removed. The tripe was then minced together with tomatoes and cereals and made into cakes.

The females got six ounces and the males eight and the food was put on top of the cages. However, if the females got easily frightened, they tended to eat their young, known as kits. Each time they heard a plane fly over from nearby Filton they would do that, so the enterprise was not exactly profitable.

We also got some pregnant sows and litters of piglets. There was a farm nearby where they made butter and we got their whey which was suitable food for them. A chicken shed was built with the eggs produced being sold in the shop. Foxes started to make their appearance so a gaggle of geese were bought in to deter them.

Here I was with a shop, a baby and a smallholding when mother came to visit us. She was absolutely horrified. Thinking back on it, I'm not really surprised. She said I didn't get married to a British army officer to end up like this.

As it worked out, the eggs paid for the feed for the pigs, the pigs paid for the food for the mink, and in theory the mink should have been clear profit.

DESPITE the onerous commitments, I still continued going to the Civil Defence and was sent to the Home Office College at Falfield to become an instructor in the HQ section.

Part of the section were intelligence officers who, with the Cold War increasingly dominating, had to record the proliferation of nuclear weapons.

There were an insufficient number of physicists

within the Civil Defence, so a number of people were selected to take nuclear physics at Bristol University and I was one of them and the only one who passed the exam successfully, becoming a Civil Defence intelligence officer.

In 1959 there was a national Civil Defence competition. The Bristol team got into the final which was held in London. I was the only person without a degree in nuclear physics but spotted the red herring that was fed to us in readings of fallout. I would never then, nor now, accept a statement without questioning it and, consequently, we won. I still have the silver shield presented to me by the Queen Mother.

By this time, Bert had retired from the army and it was a question of what we were going to do next. The Civil Defence officer thought Bert would be a useful addition to his staff except there was no vacancy. Instead, I thought that, maybe, I could find a full-time post with them.

I put in 16 applications and the bulk of them received replies that they didn't want a woman, it was the preserve of retired police and army officers.

Cousin Edith, who lived in Reading, wrote to me that there was a vacancy for an assistant Civil Defence officer there. I sent my details, this time leaving my gender out and I got an interview. Again they said they didn't really want a woman but were sufficiently impressed that I got the job, for which I was over-qualified.

DURING our last year in Downend, Stuart, who had got married and joined the Air Force, eventually got posted to Cyprus.

Beforehand, because he and his wife were too young to qualify for married quarters, they were living in a caravan, together with Ian, their young child. Bert agreed that we would put the caravan on waste ground next to our garden for which Chris dug an enormous trench, about six foot deep. Both the hole and the caravan came in very handy.

When Bert left the Terriers, we found we had acquired a big box of ammunition which couldn't be accounted for in any way. When we eventually moved, we buried the box in the trench and covered it with soil. When I recently looked on Google Earth, I saw that the spot is now covered by two semi-detached houses. I wonder if the ammo was ever found.

Soon after, Peter, Bert's adopted son left the Army and he and his wife arrived on our doorstep. We rearranged the sleeping arrangements so that they could have one bedroom.

Peter had a job but it wasn't until just before we sold Downend that they actually managed to get a house. In order to move to Reading, we sold the business but at a personal loss as, naturally, Frank wanted his share. That meant that we had to wait until the house sold before we could recoup enough money to look for somewhere else, which was where the caravan came in handy in the meantime; Chris, Pauline and I living in it in the corner of a field in Reading.

Life Four

✽

B ert, initially, went to live in Peter's new place and it took him some time before he joined us in our mobile home.

1960

I COULDN'T put the caravan onto a registered site because they would only have ones there that they owned, so we ended up in the corner of a field near Calcott.

The farmer and his wife were very friendly and fenced off part of a field. It was quite a big caravan. The main sitting room had a fold down bed and put-you-up so theoretically you could have two bedrooms.

It also had a stove that ran on coke and provided hot water and heating and a nicely fitted kitchen. Beyond that a small room with a bunk bed and a bathroom, but no toilet. We put up a canvas tent with a toilet seat over a large bucket which we tried to use as little as possible. There was quite a problem as to where to empty it.

To make it more homely, I planted boxes of geraniums around the caravan but unfortunately they proved tempting to the horses in the field. They jumped over the fence, ate the flowers, and rubbed their backs against the caravan violently, which could be rather disconcerting, especially at night. It felt like being in a ship at sea.

I did have a portable radio and the farmer put an extension of electric wire to the caravan. I had no idea whether it was legal or not, but it was certainly better than the little gas lights originally installed.

Cooking was from a gas cylinder outside the caravan. The other thing that we added was another tent outside with a shower, which was alright in the summer months. Obviously, though, only for cold ones.

WE found a house in Reading at 28 Juniper Way. There was just enough money for the deposit.

Being a woman, I could only get a mortgage if my husband guaranteed it and he only had a small army pension. Bert had been 40 years in the forces but his pension was based on the first 20, ending in September 1939, although he was called up again when war broke out and served a similarly long term. He had three days out in total and he never went out of uniform. The only person in my family living in the UK was Edith, whose mother had been my grandmother's youngest sister of eleven children.

Once we had moved in, it left a problem of what to do with the caravan, the drive up to the house was very steep and it was impossible to put it on there. We sold it to the caravan park, we had no other option. When Stuart eventually came back from Cyprus he was very disappointed, but as Bert had paid for it he thought he had the right to dispose of it.

Instead of the caravan, Eric, Edith's husband built a huge garage which could have taken two cars side by side. At the back of it was a workshop with doors leading out onto the patio. I used my knowledge of bricklaying to build the patio and the wall leading up to the garden which had quite a slope.

Chris and Bert were very keen on model railways so a pulley system was installed in the garage which allowed a huge decking to come down, on which the track and its accessories was built. The centre of the decking was hollowed out so that the person operating it could stand in the middle of the layout which also included stations, hills, roads and a whole countryside.

MY responsibility in Civil Defence was welfare, specifically, 'emergency feeding and care of the homeless' neither of which I was qualified for. I was sent to Civil Defence school at Easingwold in Yorkshire and to the Civil Defence staff college at Taymouth Castle, Scotland, because I had correctly forecast the likely questions for the written exam.

The latter was surrounded by a golf course and adjacent to a salmon river. At Taymouth Castle I was the only female on the course of 30 and I was allocated a beautiful suite of rooms. I was also introduced to single malt whisky, for which I retain a weakness. They tried to teach me golf, but after it took me 36 strokes to do one hole, I decided it was not a sport for me. It was an exciting time, not least because a number of the men were proper kilt-wearing natives.

At the end of the course there was a three-part examination; written, oral and a presentation and after we'd got through it, I had 20 tots of whisky lined up in front of me which I was expected to drink on my own! I managed eight or nine.

The Woman with Nine Lives

The Civil Defence HQ for Berkshire was at Calcot and, being an agricultural county, there were shows practically every weekend throughout the summer. At these events, a tent was put up for recruitment. On account of having to work weekends, I negotiated that I could have one day a week off and enrolled on a catering course, thinking ahead that perhaps that might be my next career.

So on Tuesdays I'd come home about seven in the evening and always brought back what we had cooked, normally three courses. Chris and Pauline always eagerly awaited my return.

THERE were 17 CD training centres in Berkshire, one of them in Windsor and the first time I went there I lost my way, as I did on every subsequent occasion over the next four years, instinct seemed to get me there.

On all the courses I attended, I finished up with distinctions and, eventually, I was called upon to take part in various Home Office working parties.

Instructors were predominantly male, mainly ex-military or police, so Lord Merton, who was national head of the body, gave me the soubriquet of Mrs. Civil Defence.

There were only two women in senior positions, the other being based in Stirling. As my section grew it was agreed that I would get an assistant so Annabel joined us.

One of my tasks was to arrange first aid courses in villages, which proved to be very popular although, on one occasion, the cowherd's wife got top marks and the Lady of the Manor failed, much to her disgust and annoyance.

WE had been in Reading about a year when the thought entered my head that it would be rather nice to drive to Spain and spend some time there. I negotiated a month's leave, much of it time off in lieu, got a green card for the car, lots of maps - which Chris and I perused avidly, currency, a Spanish dictionary and found a house to rent in Arenys de Mar for two weeks.

In 1962, driving on the Continent was rare and quite hazardous. We decided to cross the Channel from Newhaven to St. Malo and discovered that Pauline got seasick the moment she stepped on a boat. The night time crossing took several hours and while Bert and Chris enjoyed the seabreeze and spent little time in their bunks, I had to wedge Pauline against the wall and comfort her through a difficult night.

We took the long way to Spain, through Rouen and Lyons, over the Pyrenees stopping for bed and breakfast mostly in farms and buying bread, cheese and fruit in the markets before setting off on the next leg.

Bert enjoyed making fry ups on our Primus stove. He refused, however, to drive the car, an Austin estate, after he had driven round a roundabout in Lyons in the wrong direction. The trip across the Pyrenees was incredible. There were no auto routes, wild ibex roamed and hairpin bends abounded

The house in Arenys de Mar was in a side street while the main one was a dried up riverbed and, since flash floods did happen, at night the car had to be taken up to the square in front of the church. Ours was the only one with a GB plate.

We made friends with our neighbours, who actually owned the house in which we were staying. Pauline and their little girl sat with their dolls on the doorstep, communicating somehow although they spoke different languages.

There was an enclosed, paved area at the back of the house. Early in the morning we could hear lots of noise so Chris and I went to investigate and found that it was the market.

The Woman with Nine Lives

We had never seen one like it before. You could buy chicken feet by the dozen, perfect for making soup, all and every kind of fish and shellfish, oranges, odd shaped tomatoes and other fruits and vegetables, many of which we had never heard of or tasted before. We were adventurous and bought most of them.

That did not stop us having meals out in the evenings in the open-air eating places which our neighbours introduced us to. Mornings were spent on the beach and heladas – Spanish ice cream - came courtesy of wheeled stalls.

Then back to the house for a siesta, a leisurely wake-up and stroll, perhaps down to the beach, stopping on the way at different stalls, where they made fresh churros dipped in chocolate. We even had time to go further afield and visit Barcelona and Montserrat where there was the Black Madonna, always taking in the local colour and food.

We had planned to drive back via a different route. The AA had provided us with maps and directions but advised us to always observe local signposts as they would be more reliable.

We wanted to come back via Carcassonne, to Puy and then Paris, possibly also tasking in the Dordogne.

It all started out fine, until we came near to the Massif Central. Our directions said turn left, the sign indicated turn right. In accordance with the advice of the AA we resorted to local knowledge and found ourselves ever-climbing, past a mountain rescue hut and with no way of turning back.

Accompanied by deathly silence from the normally noisy children, with a steep mountainside on the left and the tops of pine trees on the right, we arrived on a plateau which resembled a lunar landscape.

There was no sign of where the road, which had by now become narrow, would lead us. Negotiating between boulders, we reached the other side and noticed a track leading downwards.

We started gingerly traversing steep, sharp bends, and eventually came to a river. I stopped the car, my hands and feet trembling, and we got out. In a layby there was another car parked and I asked them, falteringly, where we were. They, in turn, asked how we had got there and when I told them, they just shook their heads and motioned that the path was not for cars. It turned out we were in the valley of the Dordogne.

From there our journey was less fraught, Chris managing to navigate us back to the port where we spent our last francs on mussels and chips, Bert having given up.

MOTHER wrote to me nearly every month.

They were always thin blue airmail letters, typed, with not a spare centimetre anywhere. They were chatty, it was just as if she was talking to me and scolding me for not writing as frequently as she did. But I had my hands full with Chris and Pauline, Bert, a new job, new surroundings, new friends. I tried.

In one communique, she told me that she had sent a parcel of papers to a solicitor in London, and would I please contact him and arrange an appointment in connection with 'Wiedergutmachung' – which didn't mean a lot to me. It turned out that it was in connection with a compensation scheme by the German government for those nationals who had suffered under the Nazi regime.

Since I had gone to schools where the teaching language was German and had school certificates to prove that, I could justifiably claim under this law. It was a lengthy and, to me, a very traumatic procedure. First of all I had to get my doctor to provide exact details of my state of health, injuries, medications, and for him to send this to a consultant in London, nominated by the German authorities.

I was then asked to go and see him. In view of the limited movement in my right leg and my neck, results of injuries inflicted on me in Birkenau, he anticipated that I would arrive in a wheelchair. I told him that as far as I could, I would manage on foot.

Having corroborated the physical aspect, he then wanted me to see a psychiatrist. An appointment was made and back I went to London. The questions I was asked I just refused to reply to. I had, by now, worked out a system for blocking out the trauma so that I could cope and get on with everyday life.

Question after question I sidestepped.

Eventually he threw a box of matches across the room and shouted: 'I can't get through to you.'

My reply: 'I think I just got through to you,' left him speechless.

I did get a German disability pension, based on the assumption that discontinuing my education and the disabilities incurred had reduced my earning power by one third. It proved useful, it paid the mortgage.

The side effects of the proceedings were, however, nasty. Memories came flooding back. The only way I could cope was to go to London and walk and walk. Bert was very understanding, he never asked questions.

He knew the hotel where I sought sanctuary and I usually only stayed away a couple of days. I can't remember how I justified my absences from work, I certainly did not tell anyone anything about my past.

ONCE, I was walking along a street in London and saw the plate of a psychiatrist. I was feeling desperate. I rang the bell and went into the waiting room. The receptionist asked: 'Your appointment?'

'I don't have one,' I said, 'But I really, really need to talk to him.'

She looked at me and something about my state of mind must have got through to her.

'Please wait. I'll have a word,' she said gently.

She went out and came back a little later.

'He is full for today but, if you are willing to wait, he'll see you after the last patient,' she said.

I went into the waiting room and waited and waited. I found it odd that all those waiting were women. After about two hours, having looked by now through all the illustrated magazines without taking in any of the contents, the receptionist came in and took me into his office.

'What is it?' he asked.

The floodgates opened.

I can only remember that I told him about the continuous nightmares I had of things I had seen and experienced in the camp, how they came back night after night, how desperate I was, how I didn't think I could bear it any longer – and I cried, something I very rarely do.

He listened intently and after due consideration said: 'I can only see you if your doctor refers you. Get him to do that and we'll work our way it through.'

I dried my tears and replied: 'I can't tell my doctor but you have listened to me and I'll be alright now.'

I walked out of the surgery back to the hotel, packed up my things, paid the bill, got a taxi to Paddington and the next train to Reading. And that was that. I managed from then, perhaps because I had been able to share some of it.

The Woman with Nine Lives

Benji's Story

*

Being the youngest son, he was called Benjamin. There was Theresa and Isabella, then Thomas Kaufmann. Four children were enough for any family, even in the 1880s, especially in the village of Kolesd in Hungary.

Theresa and Isabella married, both of them well, and went to live in Budapest. Thomas also got married and they soon had a baby boy. Benji was to have all the advantages, he was sent to grammar school in Bonyhad and was then to go to university in Budapest and study medicine.

Thomas was to make the family fortune. He and his young bride emigrated to New York, where the pavements were made of gold and left their baby boy behind to be brought up by his grandparents and join them once they had settled in their dream home.

But dreams and reality are two different things. Grandfather died and the family had to sell the village pub because it was unheard of for a woman to run one alone.

Benji had to leave university and get a job to help

keep his mother and little nephew, also called Thomas, because the pavements of New York were made of stone and the dream house had become a little flat in the Bronx.

After young Thomas finished school he was despatched to join his parents, whom he only knew from photos and letters. He eventually became a teacher and lived in the Bronx to the end of his life. Grandmother died soon afterwards.

Benji did not resume his studies at the university because the First World War had started and, being a handsome and brave man – and also a good photographer – he became an officer in the Austro-Hungarian army. They lost the war and although glamorous, the military was not really a career for an impecunious Jewish boy. Instead, he joined an insurance company.

Not just any insurance company, but the best: Assicurazioni Generale, or Allgemeine Vesicherungs.

Czechoslovakia was a new entity and the eastern part of it, which included Ruthenia, was a largely unexplored territory. Its main city was Kosice and Benji was asked to open an office there. In 1920, he'd married Irene Elbogen and they moved there where their daughter, Iby was born.

Two years later, Irene's father Isidore's health deteriorated and she and Benji, then known to all as Beno, came back to Bratislava. The cycle business, which had started in part of the gateway of the house where Isidore and his wife Netty lived, had now grown and was a proper shop in a side road off the main street, Obchodna.

By the time the Beno and Irene's son Tomy was born, in 1929. The shop was in the centre of Obchodna and a couple of years later it moved into the Passagna, a covered shopping area. Besides bicycles, it now stocked sewing machines, prams, gramophones and their parts, as well as acting as a wholesaler to many small shops around the country. In 1941, the business was 'acquired' by the government but Beno and Irene still had to work there.

On 24 January 1942, Beno was taken to the Novaky labour camp while Irene continued to work in the shop. Released, in November 1943 Beno, his wife Irene, their son Tomy, niece Magda and Irene's mother Netty escaped from Slovakia to Hungary.

Magda's parents had been taken to the camp on transportation to Auschwitz, and Netty and Isidore had also been in Zilina. Isidore, by now in his seventies had a heart condition and serious oedema, so it was not surprising that after two weeks in the camp, he died. Irene went up to Zilina for the funeral and managed to persuade the camp authorities to let Netty out for the occasion.

After it, Irene spirited her away to a farm near to Topolcany run by John, the husband of the Kaufmann's former cook. It was now of paramount importance for them all to leave, as Netty's absence would be noted and it would not take the authorities long to figure out where the frail old lady had gone.

John had already taken Iby to Budapest by then, crawling through ditches and no-man's land at night time. But this was not something that could be done with such a large group of people or with a person as frail as Netty.

Irene contacted John and asked him to come with a lorry and take the contents of the flat and they would all hide between the furniture. John would store it all in his barn, including a suitcase full of papers and photos and then cover everything with bales of straw. John did as asked, even more he had a boat handy, the oarlocks covered in sacking.

At dead of night they all crowded into the little boat with just a few belongings and, with Beno and John at the oars, guided the drifting boat down the Danube during a moonless night.

The last part of the journey was by rail, initially to Aunt Bella's. She had been reluctant to help in the past but this was her elderly brother and family and she put them up for the night.

The next morning, the family presented themselves at the nearest police station where Beno showed them his discharge papers from the Hungarian army. Unfortunately he also had to admit that, since 1932, he and his family had held Czechoslovak citizenship.

By this time there was a steady stream of displaced people from Nazi-occupied countries and the refugee camps were overcrowded and did not want to take the children or the old lady.

Netty's distant cousin was willing to take her in, provided she would do the house work, which included washing sheets in cold water in the bathtub. Netty, who had never lived without servants had no choice but to accept. Within three weeks her hair had turned white and within six she died of heart failure.

Magda, then 13, was put into an orphanage and Tomy sought and found refuge at the Swedish embassy, still visiting his parents at the refugee camp whenever possible.

In May 1944, Germany occupied Hungary and decided that their laws on Jews, the final solution, should be implemented there.

One morning soon after, as Tomy was walking towards the refugee camp, he saw his parents being marched along the siding where cattle trucks were lined up waiting to take them to Auschwitz. The column of people, carrying small suitcases, was being shepherded by German troops and Hungarian police.

Tomy started to run towards them, crying and calling out. Beno noticed him, shouted for him to stay away and one Hungarian soldier caught him by the arm and told him to get lost, to get away, unless he also wanted to go to his death.

Crying, Tomy followed, a small distance from the column wiping his eyes and nose with his sleeve, he had no handkerchief. His father put his hand in his pocket and just before getting into the wagon, threw a knotted handkerchief to Tomy, shouting: 'Take this.'

The Hungarian guard caught it, gave it to the young teenager and told him to wipe his eyes.

Tomy turned away disconsolately, did just that and noticed that there was something knotted into the handkerchief. He did not undo it until he was safely inside the Swedish embassy.

Inside was his father's gold watch chain. Although the jewellery they had on them had been taken and the bulk left in John's barn, he had managed to secrete this one item and pass it to his son.

At the earliest opportunity after the liberation, Tomy collected Magda and they walked all the miles to Bratislava, where they met Irene who had been released from Auschwitz by Russian troops. Tomy gave his mother the handkerchief and watch chain.

WHEN I returned to Bratislava in September 1946, my mother gave me my father's watch chain and I have worn it ever since, except when the latch had to be repaired.

From ITS records it would appear that Beno arrived in Sered on 24 October, 1942.

There is no record as to when and how he left there but he was in the immigration centre in Budapest by November 1943.

He arrived in Auschwitz on 16 September, 1944, and was sent from there to the Slave Labour Camp at Muhlendorf, part of Dachau.

According to eye witnesses, he became a 'Musselman' – a soubriquet for a person who withdrew from reality and did not communicate.

He was sent back to Auschwitz on 25 October, 1944, arriving there on 1 November and was taken immediately to be gassed. Next day, the gas chambers at Auschwitz were destroyed as Soviet troops were approaching.

Life Five

✳

After four years in Berkshire, working all the hours God gave me, I thought it was time to start looking for something somewhere else.

Two jobs came up, one in Gloucester, the other in Leeds. Having been at Easingwold I had quite fallen in love with Yorkshire.

I went for the interview in Gloucester but talked myself out of it because I didn't think I liked the area sufficiently well and the following week took the train up to Leeds. I was met at the station by the then Civil Defence officer and taken for the interview at the Town Hall.

I sat on my own in an absolutely beautiful room to wait. I was then taken by the Lord Mayor's attendant to a meeting with 15 men in a semi-circle.

The job advertised only dealt with welfare, there was no element involving helping to run the HQ. Afterwards, I was asked to wait outside and then offered the post. It was almost impossible to turn it down. I was told that my salary would be doubled, they would also pay my removal expenses and provide me with rent free accommodation until I sold the house in Berkshire.

It wasn't until a year or so later that I found out I was the only person considered. I intended to spend a couple of days in Leeds to acquaint myself with the place, but the Civil Defence officer took me straight back to the station and onto the train back to Reading where I gave in my notice.

My move to Leeds opened quite a can of worms. First of all, my boss in Reading hauled me over the coals because I had not put him down as a referee. Our relationship had soured and I'd been afraid of what he would say about me. That the CDO in Leeds would phone him and ask why he was not one of my referees had not crossed my mind.

My terms of employment required three months' notice. The interview had been in March and Leeds wanted me as soon as possible. After a bit of negotiation, I eventually started after Whitsun, at the beginning of June. The others came up afterwards as Chris was finishing his exams.

I bought a nice car since the journey to and from Leeds, prior to the advent of the motorway, was strenuous. Initially I stayed in a hotel on Cardigan Road as it was near to Wheatfield House, the Civil Defence headquarters and I drove down to Reading on Friday evenings after work and back up late on Sundays. Cooking, baking and washing took up my time back there. Fortunately Bert liked ironing.

After a few weeks I rented a bedsit in a house called Throstle Nest, Horsforth. Once Chris had finished his exams, he came up and together we redecorated one of the council's more garish 'miscellaneous properties' which suited our needs at Allerton Grange Rise into something more liveable.

Significantly, one thing had changed. Between my appointment and arrival, the Civil Defence officer had died suddenly. Nobody had thought it necessary to inform me and on the first morning I turned up at Wheatfields at 8.30am, the appointed time. The place was locked up with no sign of anyone. It was not until an hour later that Harry Atkinson, the chief clerk, arrived to open and the rest of the staff started to appear.

He had no idea of who I was nor my official position. I got back into my car, drove down to the Town Hall and asked to see the town clerk, who had signed my contract. I did not have long to wait and received profuse apologies.

The now-departed Civil Defence officer had only been buried a couple of days before and besides me, there was another assistant Civil Defence officer, Alan, who had been holding the fort during the previous fortnight.

There was a slight problem, we both had the same job title and were on the same salary scale but Alan had already been there for two years.

There was not just the question of seniority but also the division of labour. It was a difficult situation, not least because Alan was clearly unhappy to have a rival having hoped to have permanently filled the senior shoes.

Personally, too, I doubted whether I could go from being a training officer to heading up the organisation in three short months but didn't make that public. Pending a decision by Civil Defence committee, we agreed that pro-tem we would each take responsibility for three sections; I had welfare, ambulances and headquarters, Alan wardens, rescue and signals.

Three months later Alan had a heart attack and finished up in hospital.

The top job was advertised and Walter Groom, who had been Civil Defence officer in Huyton and Roby got the position. I was relieved. I had been effectively flying by the seat of my pants for four months and was quite happy to return to my initially allocated duties, except that looking after headquarters stayed with me.

By September Bert and Pauline had also arrived in Leeds and we were living in Allerton Grange Rise. The house in Reading had sold very quickly, we spent Christmas with the family in Bristol and, once the builders had moved out, having laid parquet flooring and installed central heating, we moved in and contemplated what to do with the big garden, which had actually been the reason for the purchase.

Bert decided to become a gardener, in which he was encouraged by Walter. Wall, his wife Betts and Jacquie, their daughter, soon became part of our extended family. We were all strangers to Yorkshire, so had to stick together.

I HAD been invited to a regional get-together of the Women's Voluntary Service at Nostell Priory. I accepted in my capacity as acting CDO and mentioned that, by the time of the event, Wall would be in-situ and we would come together.

On the appointed day, in my best dress, we set out. Wall dropped me off at the meeting point and went to park his car. A gentleman standing there came over and said: 'I am St Oswald, pleased to meet you.'

I introduced myself, having no idea who he was. We chatted while the official cavalcade arrived and from the first car descended Lord Merton, the head of Civil Defence, who I had met repeatedly at courses and conferences at Sunningdale.

He came towards me, hand outstretched.

'Oh, Mrs. Civil Defence, and what brings you here?' He said.

'I am now in Leeds,' I replied: 'May I present Lord St. Oswald?'

'I don't think you have met Lady Reading, she is Head of the WVS,' he said in exchange.

Greetings were proffered and the group started to move towards the house.

I said to Lord Merton: 'I think I had better wait here for my boss, the new Civil Defence officer.'

'Oh no,' interjected St. Oswald: 'You come with us, my wife is from Poland and I'm certain she would like to meet you.'

So I became part of the official party, wondering where Wall was and how to explain. We went up to the house, a treasure trove of Chippendale furniture and in to the drawing room, where I was introduced to Lady St. Oswald. We talked about gardens.

'Did you know that Capability Brown laid out the grounds? Come to the balcony, you get a good view from there,' she told me.

We stepped on to it just as Wall and his colleague from Sheffield walked past. They looked up and I waved to them. Much later Wall told me that his colleague told him to watch out, because 'I obviously knew people.'

Lunch was served in a big tent. I had expected to be seated well to the bottom of the side tables but was shepherded by Lady St. Oswald to the top table, where some speedy rearrangement of seating had been done. Wall was on a side table, way below the salt.

Driving back to Leeds was a quiet affair. Wall never believed me that it was all because I happened to be in right place at the right time. My reputation was evidently made.

AT home, we came to terms with cooking on an AGA. It was rather a pain in the summer, the kitchen became far too hot, so a separate gas cooker was installed and an immersion heater in the airing cupboard in the bathroom. But in the winter months it was a godsend, except for the amount of greasy smoke. Eventually it was converted to gas.

Chris settled well into the sixth form in the new school Allerton Grange, as did Pauline at the nearby primary school.

Bert and Wall were both keen gardeners and our greenhouse and fruit cage, especially, gave them plenty of scope. Bert attended evening classes and before long thousands of bedding plants were germinated together with 72 different rosebushes. Naturally, the lawn was pristine, with stepping stones a must.

Bert was still keen on tropical fish so we acquired aquariums, one specifically for the breeding of small fry for consumption by the fancier breeds. Then we had to get a dog, there followed a couple of cats and before long white mice, guinea pigs and gerbils joined the menagerie.

Fortunately, there was a very big garage which became a home to the ever increasing number of guinea pigs. Bert and Pauline were not exactly expert at sexing and separating them.

CIVIL defence was more than a full-time job as meetings for volunteers were in the evenings, exercises took place at weekends and office work and preparation filled the days.

Our Headingley office did make it more than bearable, though.

Wheatfield House was a listed building set in a big garden, previously a gentleman's residence with even a billiard room. The orangery by its side only had the iron structure remaining, all the glass had long gone.

The orangery got me into trouble.

I was responsible for training in emergency feeding

which included building cookers from bricks, dustbins and rubble but, with the changeable weather, it was more often theory than practice.

Emergency feeding came under the umbrella of the Ministry of Agriculture, Fisheries and Food and their representative was located at their regional headquarters at Lawnswood nearby.

He frequently came over to see how we were getting on. I told him about the problem we had with practical sessions and how, in Berkshire, we had overcome that by using open-sided agricultural buildings.

'Why not do it here?' he said, pointing to the skeleton of the orangery. 'Get some estimates, it shouldn't cost a lot to put a corrugated iron roof on it, you would have your covered area and we'll pay for it.'

So I did, the prices were approved and the orangery was covered. Wall approved too, he thought it had been an excellent idea. And then trouble started.

In the attic lived the resident caretaker, who was employed by the City Council. We did not see eye to eye on many things and it must have been him who told the town clerk that we had made structural alterations to a listed building.

Neither Wall nor I were familiar with the many pitfalls local authorities had for the unwary or ignorant when we were asked if we had obtained planning permission.

'No,' I said. 'The Min-Ag chap suggested it and they paid for it so there was no expenditure for the council.'

'But that's not the point,' I was told sternly. 'Before you build anything you have to get planning permission, especially if it's a listed building and, besides, Wheatfields belongs to us so you can't do anything to it without our agreement.'

'But we didn't alter anything. The structure was there, we only covered it,' I protested.

Somehow we got away with it, and besides various groups building and dismantling cookers, it also provided a useful space for the occasional party barbecue.

THERE were two other buildings in the grounds. One was a square, heavily fortified box-like structure in which flammable material, like petrol and firecrackers, were under lock and key and the other was a newly constructed training block. It had a large space which could be made into two with folding doors, with a stage at one end and a recreation room, snooker table and bar at the other.

It became a favourite meeting place not only for the Civil Defence but for many senior officers of the local authority as well as those in the police and ambulance service with whom we had close relations.

Part of our function was to supplement their resources in case of an emergency. Since I was responsible for emergency planning, which involved the removal of women with children, upwind – mainly to Lancashire – I had to get to know Leeds in great detail.

I spent significant time driving with a police inspector along every single street in Leeds together with a copy of the latest census, to see where possible assembly points could be located, where buses and lorries might have to be parked and where the easiest exits from Leeds to the West would be. Despite its current, ever-changing nature, I still know most of the short cuts in the city better than satnav.

The core of any likely emergency feeding effort were school kitchens, which brought me into close cooperation with the Department of Education. Schools would also act as congregation places and rest centres and they would be manned and directed by social workers, so I had also to consult with the Chief Welfare officer on the training of his staff. Exercises, combining volunteers with the police, ambulance, welfare, fire and rescue and the NHS were held at least twice a year.

This was around the time of the Cuban missile crisis, when the Cold War was at its hottest.

Opposite the famous St. James' Hospital, there was a row of back-to-back houses which were due to be demolished. That gave us an excellent opportunity to test all the services in how to deal with an emergency.

The houses were carefully partly demolished, fake casualties liberally doused in mock blood strategically placed and, the fire service and rescue section the first called on to put out the fires they had started.

Ambulance and first aiders for St. John's dealt with the supposed injured and 'Jimmy's' was put on emergency footing. The welfare section was detailed to look after the homeless, who were actually onlookers, and provide a light meal and endless tea.

It was all coordinated by the headquarters section of Civil Defence with the Lord Mayor and his entourage, as well as the town clerk and all his senior officers, present to marvel at it.

We spent months preparing for the big event. Three weeks beforehand, Wall and his family embarked on a cruise, which was due to return two days before the exercise but that was fine as everything had been arranged well in time.

The final briefing, which was to be in the ex-billiard room at Wheatfields and included all the notables, together with observers from the regional Civil Defence, was scheduled for 9am on the day of the exercise.

However, there was a hurricane in the Atlantic, and

the day before, Wall's cruise liner was diverted to assist in the rescue of a ship. As the exercise approached, there was no chief Civil Defence officer. Phone calls to the ship only confirmed that it would now dock on the Monday, in Southampton.

The town clerk rang and said: 'Well, Mrs Knill, we can't call the exercise off, you'll just have to do it yourself.'

I called the other staff and explained what had happened. 'We can't let the boss down. It's all written down, we have talked it all over,' I told them.

We carried on regardless and it all worked like clockwork. Afterwards, the town clerk came over, shook my hand and said: 'Well done, I told you that you could do it.'

I LOVED my time at Leeds Civil Defence. It was as if I was being paid to do what were my hobbies, I became an adopted Yorkshire woman and made life-time friends; life was rich and meaningful.

And all this under the threat of a possible nuclear war and my passport being endorsed as not valid for travel in countries behind the iron curtain. I was also subject to positive vetting and was made to sign the Official Secrets Act again.

Bert and Wall seemed to be cut from the same cloth. They both loved sport and went together to all Leeds United matches, the cricket at Headingley and followed the 1966 World Cup all over the country. Betts and I also hit it off. We both liked sewing and clothes in general and following the horses at the races but not betting a lot.

BEING an instructor and examiner at national level, I still attended the Home Office Civil Defence staff college in Sunningdale for various courses and conferences. On one such, in early in 1967, I was told, in strictest confidence, that Civil Defence was to be disbanded and our jobs to disappear, emergency planning was to be taken over by local government.

We were allowed to tell our colleagues but not the volunteers and were advised to try and find another job in the local authority rather than be forced into the first available vacancy once the need arose.

Back in Leeds, after the shock for all had subsided, I noticed that two of the departments I had experience of dealing with, education and social services, were both looking for chief clerks. Despite limited knowledge, administration had been part of my job description and I applied for both only to find that the interviews offered were at the same time on the same day.

I tossed a coin, education won and I found myself in a waiting room filled with all-male candidates who had experience of working in the department, prior to facing a formidable panel.

After lunch we were called back in individually and I was informed: 'We have offered this vacancy to the present senior administrative officer for further education, but we would like you to let your application stand for his job.' I replied that my knowledge of FE was non-existent but was assured that they had every confidence in me.

That job, in turn, was advertised, I attended an interview and was offered the post which was specifically dealing with students' awards, a field about which I knew precisely nothing.

In the summer of 1976 I moved to education, but remained as a volunteer with Civil Defence which was not disbanded until the following year.

Civil Defence...and a woman takes the helm!

Berkshire Civil Defence, 1962. A snappy slogan!

Life Six

*

My knowledge of education was limited, to put it mildly. It mainly centred around the children. Chris had just finished at Allerton Grange High School and was awaiting his A-level results. Pauline had taken the 11plus exam and passed with flying colours.

John Taylor, then deputy director of education, advised me that she would really shine at Allerton Grange, one of the new breed of comprehensive schools, rather than at the somewhat old-fashioned Roundhay Grammar School. We lived in the catchment area for both and took his recommendation.

Higher Education was a closed book to me.

At Wheatfields I'd had a large, comfortable office of my own. Arriving on day one of my new job I found that I was to share a cramped one with three male colleagues. The next room had four females in it and there were separate windowless spaces for filing and interviewing.

All of it was in the attic at the end of a long corridor

from which other offices opened out covering various administrative duties.

My section, as a senior administrative officer, was 'Further Education: Grants and Awards.'

Student awards were subject to government regulations and case law and each year there were amendments. Some grants were mandatory for those taking degrees or degree-equivalent courses at approved educational establishments and teacher training courses.

Others were discretionary, either for students who did not fulfil the educational requirements or wanted to take other higher level courses, for instance in dance, drama, music, adult education or leading to ordination.

It took me some time to get the details under my belt. It was a minefield, especially as all parents were convinced that their offspring had every right to every course. Awards were based on parental income, except for mature students who had worked and supported themselves for at least three years.

There were additional allowances in respect of their dependants and all sorts of odds and ends. Tuition fees were not payable in those days and married women got a poor deal.

The administration of the section had grown like topsy, there was no system, it was a nightmare, local councillors and even MPs, were invoked by parents to try and find a way through the morass.

Eventually, I got it sorted, the section moved out of the cramped quarters into part of the newly built Merrion Centre and I got my own office. I was responsible for a budget in excess of a million pounds which, in those days, was a big deal.

I wasn't really happy in the work but every time I got

the itch and wanted to move, my grading and pay were increased and additional duties and staff allocated to me.

Over time, my section also dealt with further education grants, educational charities and research and development. I found myself being sent on courses and conferences, including with the Social Work Training Advisory Council at Bradford University. I could not afford to move.

GOING computerised was being discussed.

I was sent on a computer appreciation course at what was then Leeds Polytechnic and it was decided that the student awards system would be eminently suitable for conversion to the system.

I was allocated a teacher and spent a year with a computer programmer in setting up the system.

'George' a modem with access to the main computer in the Civic Hall was installed, new forms for inputting data were designed and, to top it all, local government reorganisation in 1973 meant that we had to take over awards from several local authorities. They were still on a manual system and each of their own devising.

The takeover date was 1st April, the start of the new financial year but partway through the academic year, it was not a smooth transition. I was stuck. My pay was generous but I could not move further up the promotional ladder because I had no degree.

A few years earlier, the Open University started.

The assistant education officer for FE was involved in setting it up and suggested that it would be the answer for me and better than a part-time law degree course at the polytechnic.

I enrolled in the first, pilot year and got my degree in

The Woman with Nine Lives

1973, the way was now open for me to be appointed as a principal officer in the Department of Education. How I managed to combine a full-time job, family and complete a degree course in four years still baffles me even now.

Life Seven

✻

While in Leeds Civil Defence, I had edited the monthly *Leeds Defender*, started by Wall but passed on to me after the first issue. I'd always liked writing.

I can't quite remember the sequence of events which led to my involvement with disabled people. I myself was partially disabled but managed to hide this quite successfully. My neck, left shoulder and left thigh were always troublesome. I think it must have been Arthur Goldthorpe who got me really involved in investigating the unfairness towards handicapped people.

I'd also experienced it while on the Open University summer school when I broke my ankle and had to be wheeled around by Garry, my step-grandson, from lecture to lecture and realised that people avoided eye contact and talked about me as if I was not only physically handicapped but also mentally incapacitated.

I got involved in working with and for DIG – the Disablement Income Group – becoming secretary of the

Leeds Branch. For the official opening, I invited Keith Joseph, our MP and he, the Lord Mayor and I were on the platform at the Civic Hall. I never normally wore a hat but did on this occasion and Bert, in the audience, did not recognise me.

I edited the first Leeds and District Guide for the disabled and found myself on the House of Commons working party which eventually produced the Chronically Sick and Disabled Persons' Act.

The meetings were held on Friday evenings at the House of Commons. I used to finish work early and drive down to London, usually coming back in the early hours of Saturday, having stopped at a service station for a very necessary nap on the way.

I was also asked to go to an international conference held by the Warnock Committee on Further Education for the Handicapped and found myself on an MA Course on educational management at Sheffield University.

That was a step too far and I stopped after the first year.

Life Eight

❊

Bert and I both loved music, not necessarily of the same type, but we both liked opera. When Peter Sparling, our solicitor, became involved in the creation of Opera North, Bert and I became patrons and had permanent seats in the grand circle.

We also had season tickets at the Town Hall concerts. Since Bert was tall and had long legs we had the two seats at the left end of the first row. Next to us sat Fanny Waterman and her husband Geoffrey de Keyser and then the Lord Mayor. We also had season tickets to the Leeds Grammar School concerts.

We became part of the circle of music in Leeds with all its concomitant social activities. I became a member of Leeds Piano Competition's committee, which Fanny founded, and took two weeks' leave every third year when the competition came round, ferried the competitors around and had them practice on my lovely Broadwood piano.

I also got involved in the creation of the Leeds College

of Music which at that time was just a Saturday morning school for musical children. As I had inherited a large stock of sheet music from the 1930s onwards, I donated them to the college archives.

AFTER graduating, Chris stayed on in London and got involved with researching the impact music had on severely mentally handicapped people. He met a Norwegian, Marianne, who was on a postgraduate course at the Guildhall School of Music and an exceedingly talented musician.

They decided to get married in Leeds. All the Norwegian family travelled across and after the church ceremony the party was in our garden and, according to Norwegian fashion, guests wore either black tie, evening dress or national costume.

Chris wanted to have a maroon suit with very wide trousers to match his locks and beard. No such item to be bought, so I made it as well as bridesmaid Katarina's dress. Afterwards, Bert and I went, by boat, with the whole family back to Norway.

It is an enchanting country and I have spent a lot of time there since, I even learned Norwegian. I found, however, that since English was taught in schools in Norway and Sweden from age eight everybody, including tram drivers, wanted to practice their English on me, at least in the towns.

Out in the country, Norwegian was preferred but I found, to my consternation, that there are two Norwegian languages and the one I had learned was of more use in Oslo than down in Telemark or up beyond the Arctic Circle where I tended to be.

PAULINE graduated at Leeds University in 1976 and went on to Ashford College to do post-graduate work. Her degree was in agriculture and her research was financed by the Egg Marketing Board. Before long she was headhunted and in London. At university she met Rob who was now also based in London.

IN the early 1970s Bert was diagnosed with Type 2 Diabetes. At this time treatment was not as imaginative as it is now. He was admitted to hospital with ketosis and, once his blood sugar level was stabilised, came home.

The treatment was insulin injections and a changed diet. He hated the injections and would do anything to get off insulin. Over a period of months on a very strict diet, with everything being weighed beforehand, his levels were more or less normal and the injections could be discontinued. He had to keep to the new regime which was hard for him as he had a very sweet tooth.

Bert was also a heavy smoker but refused to give up. He said that at his age, he was approaching 80, the marginal benefit of extending his life by probably only months wasn't worth the sacrifice.

I had stopped smoking in 1973 after a heart attack. Nobody talked in those days of the effects of passive smoking. Bert suffered, however, from chronic bronchitis which he was willing to put up with.

His deterioration of general health was, however, a concern for Pauline. She and Rob were now living in a shared house in London and decided to get married so that Bert could give her away. St. Matthew's Church was booked here, they found a flat in Stoke Newington, the date was fixed and all the family were invited.

It was a cosmopolitan affair, Chris and family came from Norway, Stuart and his brood arrived and my relatives from Vienna and Bratislava also came, along with Bert's family from Bristol and friends of Pauline's and Rob's from all over the world; more than a hundred guests in all.

Accommodation, the wedding breakfast and all the other arrangements were organised, it was to be a great family get together. Two weeks before the wedding, I had to see a consultant at the hospital. The results came a week before the wedding and showed that cancer had reoccurred and I was to go in for major surgery immediately.

But that was not an option. I got agreement from the consultant that I would go in a week after the wedding, by which time the guests would have dispersed to their various homes.

I spent three weeks in hospital and another week in a convalescent home, Bert went to stay with Stuart and Barbara during that time.

My GP refused to let me go back to work. He told me that I had, at most, two years to live and the stress of my job would shorten that. I enquired as to whether the Department of Education could find me a less taxing job, maybe as a language tutor.

By this time I had passed the final examinations of the Institute of Linguists but cuts were made in the Department of Modern Languages at the Poly so there were no vacancies.

In January 1981, I was offered early retirement on health grounds with an enhanced pension and a nice lump sum; after all, they did not think that I would live long so they could be generous.

In May, Bert and I went to Norway. The morning after arrival, Chris put a bag in my hands and said: 'Go into the woods and paint.' It was quite a challenge but the best medicine possible. I told him I couldn't and he replied: 'Just look at things.' He was right.

When we got back to Leeds I applied for a course at

Jacob Kramer Art College and spent, what I thought would be my last year, painting, drawing, making new friends and really enjoying myself.

I came to the conclusion that further or higher education was wasted on the young! At the end of the year I decided that what I really wanted to do was work in three-dimensions using clay and textiles.

I enrolled at Swarthmore College, spent one day a week there doing pottery, life drawing and tai-chi and also went one day a week to Otley College to learn how to spin and weave.

I forgot that I was supposed to be dying and so did my body.

WE spent lengthy periods of the winter in Spain and more time in Norway where we became part of a new family. I was feeling well but there was an underlying fear of dying.

I felt I was on borrowed time.

1982

I DIDN'T sleep well. I blamed it on the wind but then the fresh air and sun had made me tired enough to ignore that.

I couldn't sleep. I was afraid of dying. One assumes, this is natural; yet on those occasions when I was near to death I was not afraid, but at peace and accepting, maybe even eager for it.

Perhaps it was the death of the two Hungarians, so close together, in the brick yard at Szekesfehervar in which I was unintentionally involved, that sparked it all off. And also I was conscious of my heart labouring. It was tired. I was weary, yet I felt that there was so much I still wanted to do and so much undone.

It was a horrible Saturday. It had been snowing every night for the previous three days and each morning I moved the accumulation to allow the milkman to come up to the back door.

It must have been about midday when the police phoned. They had found a man dead in the kitchen of his house with an empty whisky bottle beside him and a note on the table. Neighbours thought he was Hungarian and that he had been ill for a long time.

The note could have been a shopping list, would I come over and translate it.

I explained that I couldn't get out of the house and they said they'd try to come over in the afternoon. But it started to snow again and the fog came down, so I didn't hear from them until Monday, when they turned up in a Range Rover late in the afternoon.

Terry had phoned in the morning to find out whether I needed anything. She was going to the shops and could drop anything in on her way. You always run out of those things you least expect to and I did need washing powder.

She brought it in about three o'clock and we were just sitting down with a cup of tea – Bert in his usual armchair, partially turned away from us – when the two policemen came. I took them into the dining room.

The table was covered with papers and dictionaries as I was trying to finish the translation of Chris's Norwegian book.

They showed me a piece of lined paper, torn from a small exercise book, the top erratically fringed where it had been separated from the binding.

It wasn't a shopping list. I translated it for them – loosely:

They are still trying to get me.
Now they are sending messages through the electric.
When I switch something on I can hear them.
They say:
'You thought that by leaving your country
you could evade us,
prevent us from finding you.
The blood of the innocents you killed
has soaked through the earth and will reach you.'
But I was only obeying orders.

LIFE was busy, I did quite a lot of interpreting and loads of spinning and knitting. Somehow, along the way, I had joined the Yorkshire section of the Guild of Spinners, Weavers and Dyers, meeting at the Yorkshire Museum of Farming and became its secretary.

My knitted and often hand-spun garments became really popular, were even featured on television and I had to employ others to do parts of the production. Design and final assembly stayed with me.

A few years later they became so in demand that I only had time to actually design and administer selling all over the world. It was no longer fun and I closed the business down. All the time I was aware of living on borrowed time and I didn't see why I should do anything that wasn't enjoyable.

BOTH Peter and Stuart, my stepsons, had now retired from the forces and were living in Cornwall; Bodmin and Porthleven respectively.

Stuart's daughter Debbie was engaged to be married in the spring of 1984. Bert and I were going to the wedding, as were Pauline and Rob. We rented a cottage on Hereford river for two weeks.

We thought it might be an idea to use some of the time to explore the possibility of moving down to the West Country to be nearer to Bert's family again. I thought that the Exeter area was as far as I was willing to go as there was quite a lot of musical life there and it would be half way between Cornwall and Bristol.

We had booked a room in a hotel at Exeter and were driving along the A30 when one of the tyres of the car blew out. I managed to swerve and steer the car to the roadside and was joined nearly immediately by two policemen in their car who were witnesses.

'By God, you were lucky,' said one of them, 'you could have been killed. Obviously, it wasn't yet your time to go.'

I was rather shaken. They put the spare tyre on for me and escorted us to the nearest garage, where we had a new tyre fitted and we drove on.

Next day we visited a local estate agent and arranged to view a house on the outskirts of Exeter, opposite to a boarding school and at the end of the bus route. It was exactly what we wanted, with a large shed, then in use as a photography studio, which would accommodate my loom comfortably. We put in an offer which was accepted, explored the surrounding area and on Sunday drove back to Leeds. We already had a buyer for our house.

On returning, Bert fell ill and was taken to St. James' Hospital on the Tuesday with viral pneumonia. I managed to get a message to Pauline, who was out of town, asking her to come home. Bert was delirious.

I sat by him and talked to him, held his hand but I don't think he was aware of me. The curtains had been drawn around us. Suddenly he turned his head to the other side, said in a questioning tone: 'Win?' dropped his head and was gone.

Pauline arrived too late to see her father alive, but told me that she felt it when he died. I phoned Chris in Norway next morning and he was with us the following day.

Opening Bert's box of affairs, on the top were the deeds to the double grave in Bristol, where Win, his first wife, had been buried. He requested a funeral service and cremation in Leeds with the Last Post, followed by reveille and the main farewell in Bristol.

Chris, Wall and I took his ashes to Bristol and they were interred there with all the family and his military friends present.

I came back to Leeds, cancelled both the sale of our house and the purchase of the one in Exeter. John Blomfield, our friend and GP told me not to make any radical changes for two years, to give myself time.

The Woman with Nine Lives

Martha's Story

*

Judith is Magda's daughter. Magda was my cousin, the daughter of mother's sister Janka, who perished in the Holocaust.

At Judith's wedding in Bratislava I sat next to an elderly, quiet woman. She told me that her name was Martha, that she was distantly related to the bride and she lived on her own but not quite alone.

I like ethnic jewellery. On this occasion I wore an intricate ring I had bought years before, in Israel. Martha noticed and said: 'I made this ring,' but did not elaborate. It was rather intriguing. Eventually somebody, not Martha, told me her story.

Martha was five years old when her mother died. She never even saw her little sister whose birth had caused her mother's death, because Anna, another of mother's sisters who had come from the big town, took her away and brought her up as her own. Martha only knew that she would be called Elizabeth, her mother's name.

Martha already had a brother, Alfred. He was eight years old and already helped out his father who was the village cobbler. Alfred could smooth the sides of the new soles, thread in boot laces and cut squares of brown paper from the big roll in which the repaired shoes were wrapped. He was invaluable.

The problem was what to do about Martha.

For a time they tried to rub along, father, Alfred and Martha, but it did not really work out. There was no-one to tell Martha what was right and wrong, when and what to eat or even prepare something for her, or to see that what she wore was reasonably clean. Anna thought she had done more than her duty by initially taking in little Elizabeth who might or might not live.

Nobody in the village seemed to have time or space for a little Jewish girl. The grandparents lived too far away and, in any case, they had been deported by this time and the father knew that it might not be long before they also came for him and probably also his children.

One evening he decided to take the boots he had repaired to the village priest himself, rather than send Alfred. The priest had always been friendly and he hoped that he might find some answer to the problem.

Ushered in, the priest said: 'You know your little girl is in danger?'

'That's why I have come, what can I do?' the cobbler replied. 'If she is taken away she will be lost; Alfred and I can look after each other, but who will look after Martha? What will happen to her, a motherless child?'

So, little Martha was put into a Catholic orphanage in the nearest town, where nobody knew that she was Jewish.

Life was not easy for her but at least she was safe; the priest kept the secret and the nuns protested vociferously if the police came looking for hidden children, that all their little ones were good Catholics.

When the war was over, her father and Alfred were fortunate enough to survive and came to collect Martha, but nobody else of the family was left. The parent tried to pick up where he had left off but Alfred did not want to become a cobbler and decided to go to Palestine and work in a Kibbutz. He wrote in glowing terms about the warmth and fresh air, about the oranges that grew on the trees just for the asking, about the happiness he felt to be with other boys his own age and to work diligently. So it was decided that Martha would join him, the father felt too old and set in his ways to do so.

So Martha spent her teenage years on the kibbutz not far from Natanya. When she reached the due age, she went into the army to do her national service, where she met Nathan and married him.

Nathan was a professional soldier but Martha and he made their home in the kibbutz. It was not long before they had a little girl. Mariamne was only three years old when her father went out in a Jeep on patrol with his mate. They were ambushed. Nathan was riddled with bullets and died, his partner, Mojshe, was badly wounded but survived. They were not much more than 24 years old. When Moyshe recovered, he frequently visited Martha who was desolate.

The authorities offered Martha the choice of either having a pension for life or an annuity to train for a career. Martha, who had only received a very basic education, chose the latter and became a talented silversmith and jeweller.

Moyshe and his wife also had had a daughter of a similar age so it was not unnatural that the two families continued their friendship. Perhaps inevitably, Moyshe fell in love with Martha. His divorce was amicable. Moyshe left the army, went to university to study technology and set up a study in a house on the same kibbutz. Another little girl was born and the three siblings became firm friends and remained so all their lives.

The kibbutz decided to support Moyshe in his research, it paid for him to have an assistant and a secretary, as well as a car. Martha made beautiful jewellery, which sold well for the benefit of the kibbutz. The three girls grew up and in turn, married.

After 30 years' research, it looked as if Moyshe had made a breakthrough. The kibbutz authorities were pleased that the financial outlay in supporting him over that time was going to bear fruit. But it was not to be. Research by others, who used newer data, showed that Moyshe's work was not marketable after all. The kibbutz authorities told Moyshe that they would not support his research any longer and that he had to do other work now.

One day he asked Martha to go for a walk with him. She was in the middle of annealing and told him that she could not at that moment leave, but would go in another hour. Moyshe would not wait, he walked out of the kibbutz and shot himself, dying instantly.

Martha, now on her own, stayed on in the kibbutz, making jewellery, but it no longer sold so well. Her spirit and her inspiration seemed to have deserted her.

Martha's daughter, Mariamne, had two little girls; she adored them and looked after them carefully. Mariamne would not let them use the school bus, being afraid of it being ambushed as had happened on many occasions.

Every day she drove them to school and waited for them when they left. The school bus was not ambushed but Mariamne's car got too near to a suicide bomber and she and both the girls, as well as a little friend of theirs were torn to pieces.

Martha stopped making jewellery. She barely went out and lived very frugally. She mentioned something about saving up for the airfare to visit a distant cousin in the West who was getting married, the only family she had left.

She did not talk about the past, the only thing she told people on the kibbutz was: 'I must not get close to people, I bring bad luck, everyone I ever loved is dead.'

Martha passed away. There were no mourners at the funeral. Her body lies, by her request, in an unmarked grave.

Iby's Civil Defence competition winners medal

Life Nine

*

It is five months since Bert died. Time to start thinking about what I am going to do with my life now.

1984

THE most important thing is to come to terms with the events of the past; the good ones and, what is more difficult, the bad. There is only so much baggage one can carry around without it affecting your life. But this is not an easy task.

The good things first. It is easier to recall an experience in one's mind than to write it down, particularly if it is something one has jealously guarded and held close.

In 1980, after I had been so ill and was in the convalescent home, Sister Theresa, while arranging the altar flowers, triggered it off and I told her all about it. And I cried – never so much before or ever after.

Sharing the experience took something away from me, yet it gave me something new. Rather than seeing it as being something undeservedly beautiful - because my initial reaction was how does someone like me, a sinner in every way, deserve such grace, such love, such light and this glimpse of infinite wisdom – I came to accept it. And instead of bringing it out now and then and, like a miser, gloating about that ecstasy which had stayed with me for many months, I accepted it as meaning that God was giving me the strength I needed, even if I had not yet given what He asked of me.

Perhaps He understood. Perhaps He knew that by staying, I had not chosen the easy path.

I WON'T say I tried to do good because that's not really true, I tried not to harm anyone and to use my abilities for the benefit of people and not against them. To help, to hold with open hands, although I did resent and even hate at times, the restraints of my life.

I did what I had to with a lack of patience, except right at the end. I don't know whether Bert even knew that I was with him and held him. But that chapter is over.

I always contended that we are what life has made us. The past, our experiences, responses and actions fashion us like that lump of clay that gets moulded, shaped, trimmed and fired, glazed and fired again. Sometimes it breaks in the firing or little cracks show, there are hidden faults.

My purpose lately appears to have been to keep busy at all costs. Not in any bad way, because a lot has been creative and some of it has even given pleasure to others.

I don't really want, at present, to become involved in the life of the church. All I want from it is the peace and uplift of shared prayers and of the Eucharist. But somehow I seem to have found warmth and friendly hands reaching out to me and, for the first time I find a situation – also with my friends

– that I am not always and invariably the giver. And that is a restful feeling.

I WAS in Budapest at the beginning of the war, on the run and then staying with aunt Bella. Grandmother was also there, her hair had gone quite white. My parents were in the immigration camp and Tomy and Magda must have been around, but it all seems rather hazy.

It must have happened after I had been in the refugee camp at Ricse and before I went to Szekesfehervar. I told granny that I could remember on a certain night waking up and that grandfather was standing at the bottom of my bed and we talked, it seemed quite natural to me although I knew that they were really in Czechoslovakia.

Later I thought I had dreamt it but I told her the date. She said it was the exact time he had died and that it was not surprising that he came to talk to me because I had always been his 'liebling'. I was about 18 when I spoke to granny about it and it did not seem to me anything to wonder over, I just accepted that it had happened.

IT was in Szekesfehervar and they had collected us together in the brickyard. People were lying about everywhere in the drying kilns. All had brought food with them. They gave us some too but everyone seemed to be worried how long theirs would last.

I left the five of them there. My cousin, her husband and their six-year-old daughter together with father's uncle and his wife. There was resentment that I was going to the hospital and I never saw them again.

My cousin's husband had a first child of a previous marriage who had died on her sixth birthday. He was always frightened the same fate would befall his second daughter.

It did, she went into the gas chamber with her granny, as did he and my cousin and her parents. Only my cousin's son, by her first husband, survived. By chance he had been staying with friends on the night they collected us.

It wasn't really a hospital, just another brick drying shed. We used some spare bricks to build up the outer walls to provide some shelter. All the Jewish patients had been brought from the local hospitals and also many doctors, but there were hardly any nurses, so I was welcomed. Most of them wanted to stay with their own families which was understandable. I was really on my own, so at least here I could be useful.

It was all dreadful. Patients who had been operated on the previous day, mothers with new-born babies, fractures, epileptics, every kind, type and degree of illness. We only had straw for bedding and some blankets.

People were dying all around us. I was the youngest helper there so they kept me away from the worst cases but there was no rest. We took Benzedrine to keep going for three days and nights and then we were told that we would be moved the next day.

One of the doctors made me take some sleeping pills because I was too high to rest otherwise. He also gave me two pills to keep always with me. He told me: 'If it ever gets too much, take them.'

I slept that night and in the morning found that one of the old doctors and his wife had taken their two pills and were dead. We lifted them up and laid them side-by-side in the entrance of the hospital for all to see and to say their farewells because they had been loved in the community. We hoped the guards would draw their own conclusions.

When we left the camp and the hospital was the last place to be moved, they were still there looking just like two sculptures on a heraldic tomb. I do hope they gave them a proper burial.

> *'Faith is a gift that comes; the gift of assurance that the powers of light have conquered and will keep on defeating the darkness'*
> – The other side of silence, *by Morton Kelsey*

If that is so, I have faith and belief although not in everything. I have unquestioningly accepted a religious experience but intellectually I cannot countenance some aspects of the gospels.

The peaks of memory in my childhood and early teens are not that significant. Somehow my life was so full then that I seemed to skate over consciousness. When I was in hospital in July 1982 with my second heart attack, I had a cardiac arrest after the venogram.

I can remember sitting outside the x-ray department and talking with the nurse at half-past eleven. I asked her: 'Will the ambulance fetch us in time for lunch?'

The next thing I knew I was in a bed in the coronary care unit, wired up everywhere and the oxygen mask being taken from my face, my nightdress cut open at the front and my breastbone feeling as if I had been battered.

And, just before that, walking with father along the marketplace in Bratislava. He is holding my hand and smiling and then I am by the river with another friend, whose name I then knew, but could not recall later.

The clock says half past two and on my bedside table there is a brown envelope. I pick it up and think, but my name isn't Knill and what am I doing in this hospital. I don't want to be here, it was better being with father.

I feel very lightheaded, but gradually things come

back into focus and I can no longer remember what it was he or my friend said and it is all lost again. I ache for a long time and have some terrible bruises on my chest. I am alive but four hours have gone from my life.

AM I conceited in thinking that I have something to give and that, unless I do so, this 'gift' will atrophy, as it did once before?

So far I have always trusted in God and let the wind blow me and the current take me. I attempted to mark time when evil and sorrow tried to overwhelm me and take steps forward when I felt it right to do so. I didn't try to swim against the tide.

After coming to England I was stagnating in a kitchen, children, cabbage mentality, which was expected of me. I had several breakdowns. I was also, at that time, subconsciously suppressing my war-time experiences and had partial amnesia to the extent of not being able to speak or understand German.

When I have been studying or otherwise working creatively, I have felt in good mental and spiritual health. But there were stretches when that was not possible and depression, anxiety and physical – perhaps psychosomatic – illness occurred.

Thoughts of Auschwitz and Lippstadt resurface, remembrances are coming and going unhindered, not causing any more hurt. Apprehension, guilt, resentment, anxiety, depression. But fear only started when I started to fear for my children.

I could not write down everything but I shall have to bring it out of my rag bag of a past, look at it, face up to it and put it in its rightful place and perhaps also forgive myself. Not so much for hurting others, for I always tried to avoid that, but for carelessness, casualness and self-indulgence.

I have learned one thing: you need not be afraid of silence, of solitude, because it can be used constructively. There has to be determination and not procrastination, not frittering time away with trivialities, not just filling time to make it go away; for time is irreplaceable.

My own overpowering need is and has always been to help others. To be ready to help when the call comes, as it has done so often in the past.

I must continue to write, for my own and other people's sake. God give me the strength and the right words.

THE years 1984 to 1986 are ones I really do not wish to recall.

It was a tough time of sorrow and grief not only after Bert, but also for sweet, lovely Marianne, Chris' wife who was diagnosed with a brain tumour. I spent, on and off, two years in Norway and this is not really my story but Chris's and I do not wish to write about it.

After all these years those memories are still sad and raw and need not be shared. Friends helped, they were a lifeline. But Ulefoss, especially the winter there, will remain imprinted.

I remember that we had snow throughout winter at home in Bratislava but, maybe, because as a child we take some things for granted, it all seemed different there in Norway.

First of all there were the sounds. The snow geese came in and settled on the island in the frozen river, just above the sluices of the power station. You could hear them honking in the daytime and when they are joined by Siberian swans, the crescendo is incessant. They make a sound just like barking dogs.

The Woman with Nine Lives

The island is overgrown with young larches and bushes of birch, sage grass and dried stalks of wild cotton which are capped with coronets of crystals and there are little caves and bowers everywhere.

Walking on the snow, even on the cleared road, there is a constant crunch. The texture of it is hard yet brittle and, thrown over the fields, a blanket of icicles at least an inch high.

They are light, flaky and transparent, just thin slivers which make the meadows look as if someone had just spread polished diamonds all over them.

The surface of the snow, which was previously so smooth and white is now undulating having settled and moulded itself lovingly around each furrow and yet it appears so light, as if a puff of breath could blow it away. The branches of the apple trees, previously stark and black acquire a coating, just like sugar setting when making crystallized fruit.

By midday, when the sun is out, the white paint on the wood shed, which stores the logs we stack in our arms to take back to the house, looks flaky and patchy by comparison to the gleaming snow and frost. It's as cold in the woodshed as outside.

There are frozen patterns on the exterior of the house, you can't really see them but you can feel a roughness like a man's chin six hours after shaving. The doormat, if not brought in through the two heavy pine yellow doors, one behind the other some eight inches apart, becomes frozen solid and stuck to the stone porch like a mini ice rink.

It was a place of beautiful solace amidst such personal turbulence.

IN 1988 I sold the house, disposed of most of its contents and moved a couple of hundred yards away to where I still live, a place my friends call the Tardis. The chief factor in the decision were the stairs. Problems with my left leg were getting worse and the answer was a bungalow. I got a skip and started to dispose of the accumulation of years. Every day the skip was filled to overflowing and, miraculously, by the next morning it was practically empty. Obviously one person's surplus is another's need.

I'M not certain as to when I started to translate and interpret regularly. I had been a member of the Institute of Linguists since 1980 and was on its list of qualified personnel.

If I remember rightly, the first commission of any size came from a firm in Switzerland who wanted a contract translated from Hungarian into English. It was a lengthy document and they wanted it in hard copy for which a delivery firm would come and collect.

The problem, then, was not the translating but the typing up. I knew someone whose husband was doing a postgraduate course at Leeds University who had a computer and printer. They needed it during the day, but it was free for me at night.

Once I had translated the document, I spent numerous nights on the 2kb Amstrad while everybody else in the house slept, transcribing the translation and printing it out on the continuous perforated paper then in use for computers. The payment I got for the translation enabled me to buy the computer from them as, with his research complete, the family moved to Abu Dhabi.

Because the bungalow had not yet been re-structured, I installed the computer in my bedroom, using my bed during the day as a makeshift desk which was hardly ideal or conducive to sleep. Part-time foreign language courses were a growing and profitable venture at what was the formerly

Leeds Poly and by now Leeds Metropolitan University and, before long, I was teaching Czech and Hungarian there.

Bradford University's Business Management Centre had an MBA course for foreign students, many of them from Hungary. Most enrolled on it were lecturers from Hungarian universities wanting to run similar courses back home. Although their knowledge of verbal and written English was adequate for normal usage, business and academic language was unfamiliar to them and they found it near-impossible to follow and comprehend lectures or to understand the texts, as dictionaries often gave several and sometimes seemingly contradictory definitions.

One of my neighbours was Professor of Financial Studies there and he asked me whether I would be willing to help as they were struggling in their efforts to find mutually comprehensive terminology.

For two academic years, I spent one day a week with the students explaining, translating and, eventually, producing for them a dictionary of Business English for Hungarian Students.

For the students studying Czech and Hungarian at Leeds Polytechnic there were some good textbooks and teaching materials but when Slovak was added to the mix, there was nothing. So I produced Easy Slovak for Beginners to use with my class.

After a couple of years, what had been more or less leisure activities for the students had to change and the rigours of examinations were imposed on all language courses. Whereas popular ones like German, French and Spanish had several classes and different tutors, I was the only person teaching Czech and Hungarian.

The requirement was to set four examinations at each level; written, oral, essay and comprehension as well as a mock exam and a resit, in effect 12 exams for each. As the number of students was comparatively small and the classes of mixed ability, that meant that I had, in effect, to prepare 24 exams in Czech and 12 in Hungarian.

I protested, it was far more than I had bargained for and, although an additional honorarium was forthcoming, at the end of the 1994-95 academic year, I stopped teaching.

Also by this time I had much translating and interpreting work to fit in. In 1988, I had set up a company called Language Services for Central Europe and there was, more or less, sufficient full-time work until 2008, when I thought it was time to retire – after all I would be 85 years old.

For the final four years I was a translator for the European Community, involved in formulating the protocol for entry into the EU of the Czech Republic, Slovakia and Hungary, as well as interpreting for the courts in Leeds and elsewhere. Also, by now, I had my MA and other things started to be more important.

I THOUGHT I'd be able to write it down, but then realised that there was an inherent problem – language. English isn't my mother tongue. I really don't know which language is.

I learned English in my early years, lost it more or less and then resurrected it, used it, needed it, but it was principally for facts. I never felt at home using it for emotions or feelings.

Anyway, they had been buried, disregarded, were a luxury I could not afford. Richness in or of language was neither needed, encouraged, nor necessary. Commonplace words were enough, fancy talk did not fit into my new life; things were taken for granted, gestures understood.

Bert was an expert at understatement and it caught

on. He was an old man before the word sorry passed his lips and pain was never acknowledged. His motto was 'do not complain, do not explain' and that tended to dominate the environment. It oozed into my pores and I too operated on the maxim that actions spoke louder than words, to take things for granted.

So life goes on, one step at a time, we look straight ahead, wear blinkers, take in facts without colour.

When you write and are asked to give facts, you can only cope with the past in that way. There is no place, no time for emotions. Then you find a book or a writer who uses emotions and feelings but has a sparse way of inserting them.

There are no adjectives; each word has its own weight, says exactly what it is meant to and you realise that, perhaps, in this way, you might be able to release what has been dampened down.

You try to let your words fly, put meaning into facts, let the past, the hidden memories and those emotions which have been allied to them, surface and float. So you start to write again.

1996

MY attempts at recalling the Holocaust for the Shoah foundation was a disaster. I was in no state to do an active recall and the whole thing was aborted.

The only result was that I had a tearful interview with my GP, was referred to the mental health section and I spent some months talking around rather than about those matters which had so upset me.

The advice I was given at the end of the sessions was, there is no rule which says you have to remember or recall past trauma. You have devised a system of burying it and have managed to have a successful life by putting it all behind you. This strategy has worked for you, stay with it. Should there come a time when you feel comfortable with revisiting the past, do it then, but in the meantime leave it where it is. And that is what I did. But there was an unexpected residual side-effect.

1999

My biblical knowledge was rudimentary and limited mainly to Old Testament stories which I had heard as a child. I only read the New Testament, from start to finish, after Bert had passed away and I was in the retreat house at Horbury.

I attended church regularly after then, read the lesson some Sundays and became involved in many church activities.

But that was more to create a social environment for me despite having a wide range of other interests and several widely differing circles of friends and acquaintances.

Reverend Michael Cross had brought house groups in and I found myself deeply involved in discussions; questioning, seeking and devil-advocating because for me, in spite of my deep conviction of a supreme being, there were still many imponderables.

I had been on several retreats, mainly silent ones and found them a spiritual experience and yet there were still conundrums to which I would have liked answers, there was a desire to know more, to understand, rather than to accept placidly.

The parish magazine always contained a couple of sheets of information from the Diocesan office and one day there was an article about the establishment of an MA course in Theology and Religious Studies at St. John's College, York, which would normally have been aimed only at those who were training for the priesthood.

The course was accredited by Leeds University and I thought it would suit me down to the ground. I applied giving my details including a brief note on having been at Auschwitz, but asking that this should not be disclosed, if I was accepted. As I was, at this point, nearly 76 years old and the course lasted either two or three years, depending on the student's previous education, I did not think it likely that I would be accepted.

But I was and together with 20 or so other students, most of them ordinands and all of them considerably younger, I started to attend weekly classes held at Thomas Danby College. My Open University degree, which I attained when I was 50, had sufficient relevant modules to enable me to complete the MA course looking for 180 credits, of which the dissertation would count for 60.

Each module was worth 20 so that attendance for two years, provided that the modules were at a sufficiently high level and the assignments were graded as satisfactory would give me an MA. If I did not submit a satisfactory dissertation I would only get a diploma and many of the ordinand students were prepared to settle for that.

They did not think that the taxing demands of ministry would allow them sufficient time to undertake the level of research required.

Some of the subject areas were mandatory, others optional and although I avoided rituals and pastoral care as the course wore on, I found myself getting more and more interested in the role of women in the bible who were ignored or at best marginalized. Even when mentioned, their names were often not given, except in relation to the male relatives.

I remembered having been told that in the Jewish

tradition descent went through the maternal line but tribal identity was the province of males, with a few notable exceptions.

ST. Matthews' at Chapel Allerton was originally on the main road out of Leeds towards Harrogate. There were big houses with significant gardens and large staff. The church was a very lively community and parts, including a great tower were added on to it later.

Architecturally it was a mess, although its origins went back to the sixteenth century. It was the tower that caused its downfall, it endangered its very foundations and it was decided at the end of the nineteenth century that it had to come down and a new church be built.

Land was found, money was raised and a new edifice, modern and with a separate bell tower, to ensure a similar fate would not befall the new church, was erected and consecrated in 1900, a fitting tribute to the new twentieth century.

In 1999 the decision was taken to commemorate the centenary of the church with grandiose events. No half measures, all the stops would be pulled out. Even if the present congregation bore little resemblance to and was considerably smaller than the original, the centenary was to be a major statement.

Committees and subcommittees were formed. The theme was changes over the last hundred years and, fortuitously, there were ten spaces between the tall windows, each of which was to represent a decade with a large banner and a display of the time. Church organisations and schools were each allocated a decade to work on.

The group looking after 1940–50 had to depict the Second World War and its austerity aftermath but were unsure about the theme. After much discussion and some earnest debate, it was decided it should be the loss of freedom depicted by barbed wire, barracks representing a concentration camp and a swastika.

The last proposed image proved controversial and one of the members of the Mothers' Union approached the vicar as to whether it was appropriate to have the swastika in the church at all and what the likely objections would be. Steve, having invited the agitated lady in and listened to her patiently, adjusted his dog-collar, scratched his head and suggested that a person who had been in a concentration camp and who was a member of the congregation should decide on whether or not it was appropriate.

He also suggested that the group should invite that person to talk to them about their experience. So it came about that I did something I had never done before and really did not want to do. On a Tuesday afternoon I gave up to a group of women some details of that part of my life which I had kept well-hidden.

I can remember that I could not bear to look up while I spoke, it was all too painful, the memories too raw. I didn't address them for long, about half an hour at most and when I looked up I noticed that they were crying – and so was I. I decided that I was not going to repeat this experience. The swastika stayed in the design, I felt it belonged there.

The next Sunday at church was odd. Others had been told about my talk and came over either to hug me and say thank you, or avoided making eye contact. A couple of weeks later I was asked whether I would be willing to talk to other groups of Mothers' Union members. I said NO.

I was shattered after my talk and it took several days before I was able to get a normal night's sleep and to more or less re-bury things and face getting back to my work on the

Clockwise: Mother Irene, father Beno, Tomy and Iby in 1929; Iby and Tomy Kaufmann in 1930; Tomy in the garden during the summer of that year and, *below*, Mother pictured in 1932

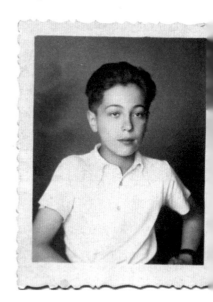

Left: Tomas Kaufmann in 1931 and, *below*, as a 13-year-old

Below: Iby and two friends pictured in 1941

Above and left: Iby's ID cards and passport she finally received in 1945

Below: Iby in Truro, 1947, enjoying the garden of Hendra Barton

Clockwise: Mother and Uncle Imre in August 1949; Iby and Stuart 1950; Stuart's wedding reception in 1956, Bert and Iby are on the far right; Iby Knill in Cornwall in 1950; Hendra Barton, Truro, 1947

Above: Taymouth Castle, Scotland Civil Defence Instructors' course in 1958

Left: Iby and Pauline Downend, 1957. *Below left*: Iby's son Chris

Below right: Entry to Guardroom of the Immigration Centre, Szablocs utca, Budapest, taken in 2010

Left: Iby revisits the Detention Centre – now a museum – in Budapest

Below: First floor Dr. Marki's residence, 27 Tokolu utca, Budapest. Both pictures taken in 2010

Left: Pauline modelling one of my designs, late 1980s

Below left: Eva and Suzie pictured in Vienna, 1990

Below: I'm a linguist!

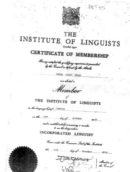

AUF DIESEM GELÄNDE BEFAND SICH
VON JULI 1944 BIS ZUM MÄRZ 1945 DAS
AUSSENKOMMANDO LIPPSTADT I DES
KONZENTRATIONSLAGERS
BUCHENWALD. 881 JÜDISCHE FRAUEN
AUS AUSCHWITZ ARBEITETEN HIER IN
DER RÜSTUNGSINDUSTRIE. ARBEITSUN-
FÄHIGE FANDEN IN KONZENTRATIONSLA-
GERN DEN TOD.

AN 30. MÄRZ 1945 WURDEN ÜBER 700
FRAUEN EVAKUIERT, JEDOCH AM 1.
APRIL 1945 DURCH AMERIKANISCHE SOL-
DATEN AUF IHREM TODESMARSCH IN
KAUNITZ BEFREIT.

IHR LEID DARF NICHT VERGESSEN WERDEN.

Lest we forget: (*Clockwise*) Lippstadt
labour camp memorial; memorial in
Szekesfehervar; memorial at Kaunitz;
memorial in Budapest on Danube

Left: Iby at the launch of Holocaust Memorial Day in 2015, with MP and Cabinet Minister Eric Pickles and Olivia Marks-Woldman, Head of the Holocaust Memorial Day Trust

Above: Iby enjoying her 70th birthday party with friends including Gabrielle de Vreese, Helen Kennedy and Sheelagh Spinks

Right: Iby's son Chris and wife Fanny, 2000

Left: Iby in 2002 with daughter Pauline and grandchildren Julia and James Ktinch.
Below: Pauline's wedding in 1980

centenary, which included researching the church's original history, trawling the records and editing the magazine. I didn't tell any of my family about the talk, it was all still too painful and I remembered, with fear, trying to recall those events for Ursula in connection with the Spielberg Shoah project a few years earlier and the effect that had left on me.

ONE particular area of the MA course had always interested me, the seemingly ambivalent relationships between David, Saul, his son Jonathan and the way women wove their way through their lives. I decided to do some research in this area and was fortunate to have Keith Wicks as supervisor, an exceptional Hebrew scholar.

I had no knowledge of the language and found, despite being a professional linguist and tutor, that the optional half-hour of weekly instruction completely impossible. He thought, and I had to agree with him, that to explore the relationship between David and Jonathan had too many pitfalls and side-tracked numerous others who had taken it on as their project.

We therefore decided that for my my assignment, I should focus on the relationship between the prophet Nathan and Bathsheba, which was not quite such a well-trodden path. Years before I had seen Alan Bennett's *Talking Heads* and I thought of using a similar method, monologues by the main protagonists plus her maid (the onlooker sees most of the picture) interspersed with short sections giving, tersely, the background research findings.

Keith liked this approach, which he felt was something new and fresh, as did the examiners.

During the second year, the question of topics for the dissertation arose. I had maintained contact with Keith and he thought the enormous amount of research I had done and the unused material I had accumulated for the previous module could be utilised in my submission which was eventually titled: 'One country (Judea), two kings (Saul, David), three women (Merab, Michal, Rizpah)'

The last compulsory module of the taught course was, topics in Christianity. Our usual tutor was by now in poor health, I don't think our relentless questioning and non-orthodox attitude helped, and another one took most of the sessions, which affected continuity.

The topic of one session was sin and evil, how to differentiate between the two, where does personal forgiveness come into it and what should be our response towards them.

Personally, I felt that any deed one could imagine oneself perpetrating in a worst moment could be classed as sin and therefore considered for forgiveness. Evil, on the other hand, was something so heinous it transcended the individual.

It was a simplistic approach and I immediately wondered whether if someone was trying to, say, protect their children at all costs, the line between the two would be blurred. There were about 20 students in the tutorial group and one of them asked: 'And where would you put the Holocaust?'

None in the room, including the tutor had any knowledge of my background. The tutor replied: 'Only a person who had experienced it could answer that question.' A lingering silence ensued.

It was a tricky situation for me. To remain quiet was to join the list of deniers, but what would be the effect of me admitting that I could answer that question?

There really was no option. I said: 'I was there'.

There were gasps as everybody turned towards me.

The tutor asked me whether I could tell them of my experiences.

'No, I can't, but I'll answer questions, as far as I am able to,' I replied.

Fortunately, the inquisitions were not about what I had experienced or witnessed but about the effect events had on my faith, if indeed I had faith before or after. I can't recall my exact answers, I was concentrating too much on being factual and truthful, on not putting hindsight on events and feelings.

News about it did, however, get back to St. John's, somebody had been taking notes and I was told later that my testimony, if you could call it that, was now part of the syllabus. Did I imagine it or did people on the course look at me differently after that?

Keith heard about it and said that I had to write it all down.

'I can't do that. When I tried to remember things a couple of years ago I had to be treated for nearly two years by a mental health team,' I told him.

'Yes but you have a promise to keep, haven't you?' he replied. 'I'll tell you what, we'll do it together. I'll hold your hand, with your best friends to support you.' I agreed, reluctantly.

So, in small stages, about 500 words at a time, taking sometimes weeks to go over one small incident and doing it slowly, like dipping my toes into ice cold water, I started with memories of my early teens.

I had already written lots of little stories about my childhood, of happy times. Gradually, that feeling of joy, disappeared as small, increasingly painful events were recorded. The steps forward got smaller and some events I just had to skip over and they are still hidden. I shy away from them even now, I refuse to acknowledge their existence in order to cope.

When I reached 1st April 1945, liberation in Kaunitz I thought that I was done but Keith insisted that this could not be the end of the story that I had to take it forward at least until my arrival in England.

That was easier writing but I needed a neutral environment for it, a space in which I could detach myself from the present and I found it at Holy Rood House at Thirsk. My desk looked out over the gardens, I was fed and watered, looked after physically and spiritually by Elizabeth and completed the task of recording coming here. It was not the end of the story, more like a semi-colon, but it had to do.

Having written it, I put it away. I did not want to read, correct or edit it. I had done it, it was now down in black and white. In between, I got my MA with a distinction on the dissertation about Saul, David and the women they shared.

Then Keith died.

2003

I WAS 80 and throwing a party. I made a speech.

'Welcome! How nice to see you all! I am so glad you could make it and come to help me celebrate this special birthday.

You may wonder why I have made an occasion of this since most people at my age prefer not to be reminded of it. But I have never thought of myself as being of any particular age and I never thought that I would live this long.

The first part of my life – a time of which I am a witness and a victim of events – made me feel that there was no likelihood of me even reaching the age of 25 but, when I did, I determined that I would cease to be a victim.

I chose a new, a different, life, to live in another country, another culture and I intended to cut off the past with one stroke.

But I had learned that knowledge and learning are invaluable. You can never know or learn too much. To prove this, I got my BA at the ripe age of 50 and my MA just before reaching 80. There were many other courses and activities from which I benefited and not all my learning or knowledge was of the academic kind.

I had a great variety of jobs and careers and each one added useful knowledge, even if only to help me to stand up to Anne Robinson.

I have never been averse to learning from others, including my friends and family, and most of you here have, often unknowingly or unwittingly, been the source of a piece of valuable knowledge on how to, or not to, do something.

And I have not finished yet, there is still so much to learn, so much to do. I have enough plans to last another lifetime!

I have certainly experienced life's rich tapestry and its richness is due to the people I have come across. Many members of my family and some of my best friends are no longer with us.

But why celebrate at all?

Well, Bert, my late husband, loved parties and was, to his last days, the life and soul of any celebration – I never got a look-in!

Bert died in Leeds in May 1984. It had been his wish to be buried in Bristol and so the family and friends gathered there. After the service we all adjourned to my niece's house in Fishponds.

I had been cooking and baking for days. Just as well,

in view of the number of people who turned up. It was a beautiful, sunny day. The crowd spread into the garden and the adjoining park and before long Bert's deeds and misdeeds caused a lot of hilarity. It was a superb party and I was sorry Bert was not there to take pleasure in it but perhaps he was, in spirit.

So I decided I wasn't going to miss out, I was going to have a big party while I was still alive and able to enjoy it. So make this a good party – a party to remember!'

2005

SOME things are long in the planning. That must have been so in the case of the 60th anniversary of the liberation of Auschwitz by Russian troops on 27th January, 1945, which is commemorated now as Holocaust Memorial Day.

In November 2004, I received a letter from the Home Office addressed to me in my maiden name which I had not used since 1947, asking whether I would like to take part in a reception at St. James' Palace to commemorate HMD.

It was to go under the title of, 'survivors, liberation, rebuilding lives' and it was not only for those who had been released from the forced labour and concentration camps but also any who had hidden in ghettos or came with the Kindertransport to England. Those involved in the actual liberation, were invited too.

I had mixed feelings. I always considered that part of my life as being the past and, as such, best not remembered, even if it could not be forgotten.

Helen, an old friend of mine, aged 93 and originally from Hungary, had also been approached and told me that she would only go if I accompanied her, which was understandable in view of the frail state of her health. So the decision was more or less taken out of my hands and I agreed to go.

After a lot of correspondence, the official invitations arrived at the beginning of January. The reception was to be followed by a commemoration at Westminster Hall and I could invite a guest to that event. To my surprised delight my granddaughter, Julia, aged 13, asked to come.

As it was going to be a long and arduous day, we travelled down to London on the previous one. Hotel arrangements had been made for us by the Association of Jewish Refugees.

Early next morning a Home Office coach picked us up and deposited us in the forecourt of St. James' Palace.

After a careful scrutiny of invitations and personal ID documents we were ushered into a large make-shift cloakroom. It had to be big, 600 people had been invited to meet the Queen and Duke of Edinburgh, whose mother had hidden a Jewish family during the German occupation of Greece and is remembered by a plaque at Yad Vashem, the Holocaust Memorial Museum in Jerusalem.

Each group had been allocated to a certain room in the palace and we were in the picture gallery, under the portrait of Emperor Rudolf II of Austria, which I thought quite fortuitous, as I had once researched his life and court. A running buffet was provided but most people were too excited to do it justice.

At 11.45am we were told to get into our groups, each consisting of 20 people. Half of the group would be presented, either to the Queen or the Duke. I stood behind Helen's wheelchair but she was not too pleased that our side of the room was to be presented to Prince Philip. She wanted to speak to the Queen.

The royal couple were running late. Ours was the last

room and they had by now met 400 people. The Queen, dressed in a simple blue, grey and black tweed dress with her usual rows of pearls was as dainty and quietly spoken as I remembered from previous occasions when I had met her.

The Duke had aged much more and his face could best be described as rugged.

Although I was not supposed to be presented, when he came level to me, he asked: 'Are you a pusher or a survivor?'

I told him I was both so he stopped to chat. He asked where I had been, I told him Auschwitz and the slave labour camp in Lippstadt. He queried whether we did forced labour there and what it was. I told him we made ammunition. Then it was the turn of my friend.

The Duke moved to the next group, all men and I think that he felt more at ease with them than with us ladies.

Helen was determined to be presented to the Queen. She got out of her wheelchair and sidled up to the lady-in waiting, who was wearing a large white hat, a few steps behind the monarch. She touched her on the arm and said: 'I was in Auschwitz and want to meet the Queen.'

She was led to Her Majesty, attempted a courtesy and said: 'I was in Auschwitz and want to thank you for letting me come to England.' The Queen not only shook her hand but touched her cheek and smiled at her. Helen never forgot that.

Next we had to get from St. James' Palace to Westminster Hall before the Queen arrived there. We had to wait in the stunning armoury until she had left for her private apartment, then join a scrum to get our coats before boarding the coach.

We arrived at two o'clock and my granddaughter and all the other guests were already seated. By half-past the

Queen and Duke arrived, accompanied by the hosts of the event the Chief Rabbi and Susan Pollack.

Besides the Queen, Tony and Cherie Blair were there, along with the Conservatives and Lib Dems leaders, the Archbishop of Canterbury and other church representatives. It was regretted that Muslim officials boycotted the occasion.

There was a lot of beautiful music including a premiere of the oratorio Annelies, using words from the *Diary of Anne Frank*; the Boros Gypsy Ensemble and the choir of the Central Synagogue beside the Royal Philharmonic Orchestra, and a cello solo by Natalie Clein.

Christopher Ecclestone, Lord Winston, Stephen Fry and Sven-Goran Eriksson spoke, as did Dr. Jonathan Sacks and the Prime Minister, all movingly.

Extracts from a film showing the return of Susan Pollack to Auschwitz and Bergen-Belsen were projected, as well as some photos which had been taken at the time of liberation. Grandchildren of survivors read out names of children who had been killed in the camp.

A flame, which had been lit some days before at the Holocaust Memorial at the site of the Bergen-Belsen concentration camp, arrived and the Queen and Duke lit from sixty 60 other survivors to commemorate the years that had passed.

It was a very moving occasion, the highlights of which were shown on BBC2. Later on I thought how sad it was that nobody I had known was there and that on numerous visits to my old home town I hadn't met anybody either who had shared my experiences and had survived.

I felt very alone. I wondered, whether in ten years' time there would be anyone left to remember; whether the memory of this inhumanity would remain or be conveniently forgotten.

My granddaughter's comment to my daughter afterwards was: 'How fortunate we are that Oma (as she called me) survived. Neither of us would be here otherwise. I want to be a human rights lawyer.'

The final word, however, belonged to my eight-year-old grandson, who watched the televised event. Turning to his mother he said: 'I don't understand it – all these people – they were not fighting the Germans, why did they kill them?'

2006

CAROLYN wanted to read the manuscript and so did some of my friends, but I was wary of letting others read something I could not bear to read myself. I was not prepared to answer questions or to face a possible difference in their behaviour towards me. It was all raw stuff, uncensored.

Helen, in particular, wanted to read it but she was still so emotionally involved in her own experiences that I felt she was the last person who should. She was bound to comment and want to discuss it and I was not prepared for that. She died a year later and never did turn one of its pages. But she thought that her friend, Edna Healey, might be interested.

I selected three chapters, none of them with 'horrors' in them and sent them to her, asking for her candid opinion. She wrote back, very kindly and suggested I should approach her agent.

I sent the same chapters to him but his reply was that he was about to retire and was not contemplating taking on any new authors. He suggested, however, two other agents, both of whom declined to take me on. So the manuscript went into a box and stayed there for another year or so.

Then Rachel came along and wanted to read it. She had no baggage and I thought that I might get an unbiased opinion. At this stage I decided to change the sequence of the book and, instead of starting with my childhood, as one would in a conventional autobiography, I placed that at the end of the manuscript and put the pages describing my escape from Slovakia to Hungary first, then went on until my arrival in England. A sort of recollection.

My provisional title for the book was 'The past is other countries.' After all, it had been an odyssey.

Rachel thought that there was just one possible title for it, 'The woman without a number' and that is what it became. She suggested some minor amendments, some of which I incorporated, but I was in two minds about the manuscript; on one hand I would have loved to have seen it published, on the other I felt that it was a self-disclosure that I was not ready for.

By this time I had joined the Leeds Writers' Circle and had read and submitted several of my short stories, with encouraging comments about how they were good enough to be published. Writing is for me comparatively easy but to sell myself or my work makes me cringe.

Ted Merriott who was the chair of the Writer's Circle at the time offered to do an edit of the manuscript after I had read a couple of chapters at meetings. I'd also met up with Bernice, of the Holocaust Survivors' Friendship Association and, through her, with Trude Silman and John Chillag, as well as with Eugene Black.

After a couple of weeks Ted returned the manuscript.

'I'm sorry, I could not edit it,' he said.

'Oh, my God, is it so awful?' I replied, somewhat surprised.

'No, not at all. I got so caught up in the story that my critical faculties went to sleep.'

The chair in the next year also read it and came up with the same response. Rachel sent the manuscript to another agency who felt that a complete re-write of the story was necessary if it was to appeal to the mass market.

But I was not really concerned with that, basically I felt that I just wanted somebody, anybody to read it and to confirm what I had felt inside me since childhood, that I could write the sort of stories people wanted to hear and read.

I knew that I could sell ideas and products if I believed in them, but there is something in me, some remains of inner insecurity, of years of being put down and denigrated, that prevented me from standing up and saying: I can write, I am good at it, I have something to say – so publish me!

In today's climate when small publishing houses have been swallowed up by the few giants whose aim it is to sell discounted books in bulk on supermarket shelves, it gets more and more difficult to get out there. I look at the rows of books on my shelves, printed in the 1950s, 60s and even 70s and marvel how they got discovered in the first place and even reprinted.

I put my book on the back burner and just got on with writing and enjoying the creation of short stories. I do like the discipline of a short story, to the point, no wasted words, no mawkish adjectives. Writing essays for my OU course in the '70s certainly honed my style.

I seem to have so many friends who have had odd experiences, unusual lives, that it seemed a pity not to get them on to paper. I began to write up some of them, fictionalising the elements.

There is an old German saying, 'Mein Herz ist eine Murdergrube' which, roughly translated, means 'my heart is like the grave dug by a murderer.' In other words, whatever you tell me stays hidden. I have always lived by that, so those stories I wrote had the characters suitably disguised or they and the protagonists were no longer alive.

Other writing forms also intrigued me.

I am no poet

I don't do poesy – don't know the rules
Of rhymes, rhythms and alliteration;
Don't know if sense or sensibility
Or even meaning is essential?

I wonder is there something ethereal,
A cloud, a dream, a wisp, a wish
To escape from mundane matters
A pre-requisite to poetry – I mean poets?

I've tried so hard to follow the rules
Have read the books, including
Exercises devised by Fry, they remind me
Of my physio – bend here, bend there.

I play with words, but not with adjectives
(The tools of lazy minds);
Give weight to sound and tones
Create a balance – does this make poetry?

I paint with words, their colours blending
Strokes on paper, telling tales, remembering
The past as it was or could have been
And the never-never land in my mind.

The Woman with Nine Lives

I tell stories, toss words in the air,
A juggler, different shapes and sizes
Letting them fall on paper, a pattern
But I've come to the conclusion that I'm no poet.

PS
Yet – has the poetry bug bitten me
That I write in verse?
Or is this even worse?
I don't want to be a poet!

2008

THE first green shoots appeared towards the end of 2008, when I was asked to speak at the Holocaust Memorial Day event at Huddersfield. I hadn't talked about the details of my experiences in the camps and was initially reluctant to air them in public.

A compromise was reached, I would answer questions only. I thought, nobody I know will be there, Melodie was coming with me to give me mutual support and I relied on Kim to look after me.

I usually concentrate to such an extent on the questioner that I am not conscious of my replies but I think it went down well. At this stage I only knew a few people in the Holocaust Survivors Fellowship Association and my connection with the Association of Jewish Refugees was also tenuous. I didn't feel that I actually belonged in either set-up.

The then chair of the HSFA and its education committee were working on a lottery-funded project 'Building Bridges.' I had already been interviewed a year before by Bernice in connection with the previous project, *Making a New Life.*

I had told her a lot, but could not bear to tell her details of my life in the camp and gave her a copy of the manuscript instead.

Sometime after the HMD event, I was asked whether I would be willing to talk at Askham Bryan prison for women on the subject, 'From Passover to the Last Supper'. My theology background was helpful and no reference was made to my Holocaust experiences. After the talk, I was asked whether I minded the chair telling the audience something about me which resulted in questions about my past.

It opened eyes to the effect such reminiscence could have and the organisation asked whether I would be willing and able in the future to become actively involved in the Holocaust Survivors Friendship Association and, in particular, Holocaust education. I had made it clear that I had a diverse and active social life and that a monthly get-together with other survivors had no appeal for me.

My Jewish roots were tenuous, to put it mildly, and I felt little affinity with the aspect of orthodox outwardly visible signs of British Judaism that I saw in Leeds or London.

To me, who had been singled out in Czechoslovakia, it seemed so odd, why be so different? Religion and faith were for me an internal issue, not something to be paraded. It had been bad enough wearing a yellow streak on one's back but these people had never been exposed to this so why? There is no answer to this I fear.

Then I was asked whether I'd become a member of the education sub-committee of HSFA, as their educational specialist had moved away. I did not think that a monthly meeting would encroach too much on my other activities so I agreed.

It was at the third meeting I attended that the chair proposed some changes to the HSFA's organisation and how the lottery-funded project might be run but, although they would have made sense in a business environment, they seemed to conflict with the rules and guidelines of the Heritage Lottery Fund. Several of us voiced our doubts.

I had not appreciated that by agreeing to be on the education sub-committee, I had also become a member of the HSFA's full committee and one of its Trustees. Eventually, I was asked whether I would be willing to chair the education committee and to work with Tracy and Emma who had been appointed to bring the project to conclusion. Lilian Black became the new chair of HSFA.

2009

FOR the previous three years or so I spent a lot of time going through the *Writers' Handbook*, trying to find an appropriate agent for my book.

I'd initially had an approach from a publisher in York after an article had appeared in their local newspaper about me being awarded an MA in Theology at York Minster aged almost 80 and that I was now writing my autobiography. The book had only just been started at that time and publishing was not something on my mind then.

In the summer of 2009, Trude Silman sent an email with news of a competition by the BBC, which was trying to find the best personal stories in the UK over a range of categories including survival. My friend had submitted hers about being a refugee child in Britain and thought that I might be interested to send in mine or part of it.

I had a look at the website – several times.

There were some really moving stories, some funny ones, some disturbing ones, none about experiences of the Holocaust and I wondered whether mine would fit in. They were all British-based and told about events affecting people living in and from the UK, my story was so different.

The web page asked for a summary of 300 words and a 2000 word extended version. The synopsis I had prepared some time before which was double in length required could be abbreviated, but 2000 was going to present me a problem. During the OU course I had found that this particular length was hard to achieve and do justice to. To extend something, which sat at 1,500 words never produced a result that pleased me and cutting down from more always seemed to me to leave out some essential parts. But there was no option if I wanted to be considered so set about it.

The problem was, the initial 300 words gave the bare facts of the period 1942–45. It told nothing about what happened afterwards, nor about my childhood or my family and certainly and, most importantly for me, nothing about what I had started to do in the last year, which had made me face up to the past and how I was starting to repay the gift of life by sharing my experiences with students and young people.

The purpose of the manuscript had been to leave something tangible to my grandchildren, to provide them with some knowledge about their roots. We all need them to give a basis from which to grow, to allow us to understand who we are, why we behave, act and react in a certain way. Yes, upbringing, nurture, parents, circumstances all contribute, but we disregard our roots at our peril.

So I set to crafting something representative and it took time. Eventually I had produced exactly the 2,000 words, as required. Now all that remained was to get the two parts on to the BBC website before the looming deadline. I tried and tried again and either the website or my system crashed, repeatedly. The deadline was midnight, maybe it was not meant to be submitted. Half an hour before the appointed time, I managed to send in both parts, sat back relieved and forgot about it.

About three weeks after the deadline, I looked at the BBC *My Story* website, but there was no sign of mine. I assumed it had probably arrived too late for consideration. It did not seem important, life was busy, anyhow. Then I had a phone call. Did I know that about 8,000 stories had been submitted? I confessed I didn't. The first selection had been done and my story had made it through.

'How many is it down to now?' I enquired.

About 4,000 I was told. Again I didn't think too much about it. Another phone call said your story is now in the top 1,000. I thought good, but nothing to be excited about.

Phone call after phone call. 'Your story is in the last 28, 15 will be selected; three in each category. Can you come down to London for an interview and to be filmed?' said someone on the other end of the line.

Now things did get exciting. The BBC specified the date, sent me a ticket, told me where near Paddington I would be picked up and who would be my contact. Come the day I boarded the train and found that, to my consternation, I was on the wrong one, it was going to Scotland.

The ticket collector advised me to get off at York, change platforms and catch the train going to Paddington. It arrived early, only 10 minutes after the one from Leeds and the taxi was waiting for me.

I had been told to bring identity documents. They were checked and I was asked whether I would agree for somebody to write my story, should I be in the last 15. Consternation ensued when I told them that I had already written the story, it only needed publishing.

I can't remember who was on the short-list panel, except Kate Mosse. They were lovely, although the next step was that I had to be interviewed by a psychiatrist to ensure I would be able to cope with the trauma of the publicity and everything else that might go with it. Within a few words we discovered we had friends in common, his wife was a pianist and I was on the committee of the Leeds Pianoforte Competition. We talked about music.

Suddenly he said: 'Good God, there will be a queue of others I have to see and we never talked about the things we should have. Here, take this questionnaire and complete it in the waiting room then give it to my secretary. I'm sure you will be OK.'

The taxi that had been waiting for me took me back to the station and this time I got on the right train to return to Leeds. I contemplated all the way back. I'd been told that if my story was chosen I would go with a camera crew to Germany and Hungary to film the story.

Was I excited? Yes and no.

To get the book published, which was part of the deal for the top three selected in each of the five categories, would be nice, but did I really want to revisit those places which brought back painful memories? The one thing I was certain about was that under no circumstances would I go back to Auschwitz-Birkenau. Other places might be okay.

A week later I was told that I was a finalist in the survivor genre and a packet of contracts arrived for me to sign. One for the BBC, which precluded me from contacting anyone else with my story for nine months after its showing, another with a publisher and a third with an agent.

A time scale was included and, on the proposed date, I was to go with a camera crew and Frank Gardner to Hungary and Germany. A few days beforehand, an Icelandic volcano erupted and all flights were cancelled. Panic set in for the producers. All the other stories had been filmed and edited bar mine.

Eventually the air cleared and I, together with the film crew, left Gatwick for Frankfurt. Frank Gardner was to join us there. From Frankfurt we would go to Kaunitz, the place where I had been liberated.

An advance party had been to Germany and Hungary to explore the sites and to get agreement for filming. The owners of the site of the slave labour camp in Lippstadt were unwilling for any filming to take place there, nor were the authorities at Kaunitz helpful. Thinking back on it, and in view of my subsequent experiences, it is possible that the wrong people were approached, because in later years I had meaningful and friendly contact with people there. And in 2015 two long articles about me and my book were published in Lippstadt.

The Hungarian authorities at the brickyard in Szekesfehervar were more than helpful, but the factory itself no longer existed. It was one of several which had outlived its usefulness. But there was a caretaker and he gave me a brick from the original works. The camera crew managed to bring it back to the UK and I have it still. The hospital wing is still there, beside the disused railway line.

Szekesfehervar did not forget the 3,000 Hungarian Jews who were taken on 12 June 1944 to Auschwitz. In the centre of the town is a memorial on the site where the synagogue once stood, brass nameplates of the 290 who returned are embedded in the square and a memorial chapel, near the Jewish cemetery, where unfortunately many tombstones had recently been defaced, gives the names of all those who did not return.

Those of my father's uncle and aunt are there. I

should have checked whether my name was also inscribed because I did not return either, but for other reasons.

In theory, I was supposed to have a free half day with the crew to take photos of places of particular interest to me, but those organising our flights had no idea of the distances involved and how long it would take to get from one place to another. That did not materialize and we were unable to film anything in Budapest.

As it was, we got to Ferihegy, Budapest Airport, minutes before the flight was due to leave. Fortunately, it had been delayed as the incoming plane had not yet arrived. We landed, I got a taxi to Kings Cross and caught the train to Leeds with eight minutes to spare.

Frank Gardner and I got to know each other on the trip. It's a small world; his father had been with the military government in Germany at the same time as I was and not far away either. He had probably frequented the same officers' club at Lippspringe, and his mother had worked in the British Embassy in Budapest.

Because of the long travelling times between the different sites, there were big gaps in the eventual film which were filled with archive footage of the Holocaust that had nothing to do with me. And the four or five days shooting out there resulted in a film of about eight minutes.

I felt disappointed that we had not been able to visit and record those places which were important to me in either Budapest or in Szekesfehervar. I spoke to Chris and Pauline about it and we agreed that it was important for all of us that the story should be complete. We decided to fly to Budapest, Pauline and I from London and Chris from Oslo and meet up there.

I booked us into a nice boutique hotel in Váci utca and we started our explorations. The weather was beautiful, my

The Woman with Nine Lives

Hungarian was still accent-free and the food at a nearby restaurant was really good.

We arranged for the hire of a taxi for half a day. First stop was Garia utca, where Marton had lived. The old house had been demolished and there was a new apartment block in its place. We had better luck with Aunt Bella's address. The house was still there, geraniums on the balcony on the first floor. But, the gate was closed and there was no way of getting into the central courtyard from which the inner balconies to the flats opened but we took a photo of 21 Jozsef korut anyway.

Next, we tried to find the immigration centre in Szabolcs utca. The concierge had assured us that it still existed but it turned out to be in the grounds of a hospital which had been closed down. However, as it was deemed to be a place of historical interest, the whole site was enclosed in a high wire fence. All we could see was the dilapidated wooden guardhouse, which Chris duly photographed.

The next stop was to find Dr. Marki's flat. Again we did but could not get access into the inner courtyard and the ground floor was now a Chinese restaurant. I stood at the corner and said: 'The church where I was baptised was just over there' and turning round, I saw a spire but it did not look right. I asked the taxi driver whether it was the Andrassy church.

"Yes", he said. 'But there was a fire and they had to rebuild it."

We drove to it and found workmen busy inside and also many women cleaning and polishing. It was all so bright, so different. One of the women came over and I told her why I had come.

The welcome I received was overwhelming, the old cross was still there and so was the layout. I did not ask after

Father Andreas, it was a lifetime ago, there was no chance of him being still alive. I spent a quiet, reflective time there.

We then tried to find the Detention Centre. The taxi driver assured us that there was no problem as it was now a well-known Police Museum but it still looked forbidding.

There was still time remaining on the clock and he offered us that, since we had paid for him, he would take us on the tourist trail, over the bridge, up to the castle and the lovely view across the Danube.

Coming back along the side of the river, I suddenly spotted 'the shoes', a memorial to the thousands of Jews who had been shot by the Nyilas as the Russian troops approached the city. We stopped. There was no need for plaques, we all knew what they represented. The picture we got of them always ends my talks now, to remind people that you did not need to be German to be a Nazi, to be anti-Semitic, to kill people just because they belonged to a different religion.

The next day we drove to Szekesfehervar, to the town centre to find the jewellery shop which had been Ella's husband's, to find the memorial in the unnaturally immaculate square with the names, in brass, imbedded in the pavement. Everything was so clean, everywhere so different, sanitised.

We visited the market in Budapest on our last day to buy presents, to relish the multi-coloured fruit and vegetables, to eat real Hungarian food and to listen to a traveller's band playing my father's favourite song. We wanted to leave Hungary with a good feeling, with kind memories and we did.

In 2013, Robin Pepper, a student at Teesside University, made an 18-minute film about my story for his dissertation. I think it is much better than the BBC version, you can get a link from my website or on youtube.

PART of the overall deal was the publication of my book on the same date as the film was to be shown, 5 October 2010. But, in the July, I had a distraught phone call, the publisher had refused to publish a Holocaust story, he did not consider it marketable. I was told that, as a consequence, the agency had also withdrawn.

'Tear up all the contracts, you are free to get your book published by any publisher, but it must not be before the date of the film. We are really, really sorry and will do anything and everything to publicise it and your story,' the BBC said. As it turned out, only the overall winner's book was ever published under the original agreements.

I had spoken at the Holocaust Memorial Day in Leeds in January 2010 and was approached by Phil Caplan of Scratching Shed Publishing after my talk. 'Had I thought of writing my story?' he asked. If so, he would be interested in publishing it. I explained the situation and that I was contracted to another publishing house.

But now the way was clear. I contacted Phil and got the manuscript to him. Hectic editing, revision and design followed and *The Woman Without a Number* was published on 8 October 2010. To say that the short BBC documentary and the publication of my book changed my life would be an understatement.

THE last five years seem to have gone so quickly and have changed things so much that I can hardly credit it. The changes were not only external but also affected me deeply.

Since January 2010, I have kept a diary of the events at which I have spoken and the number of people I have addressed, it is a phenomenal amount and shows no signs of slowing down.

By the time that 2010 came around, my name had become known through the Holocaust Survivors' Friendship Association.

Looking through my schedule of bookings, that month alone I was on Radio Leeds, ITV's *Calendar*, had spoken at the Holocaust Memorial Event at Leeds Town Hall, at the Victoria Theatre in Halifax and at Huddersfield Town Hall, as well as Trinity University in Leeds and St John Fisher High School in Harrogate. There were 26 more locations that year.

In 2011, I addressed the Speaker's House in the Palace of Westminster, talked at the Royal Overseas League's Princess Alexandra Hall in London, the UK Youth Parliament, to Rotaries in Scotland; altogether at 43 locations.

The following year, I added the UK Youth Conference on Democracy where I was the closing speaker, followed in 2013 by the Guild Hall in Hull, the Council Chamber in Chesterfield, Teesside University and also a Skype conference with a college in Iowa, USA and an American School in Germany.

In 2014, Jeremy Vine on BBC Radio 2 interviewed me, I spoke at Putney High School in London, at the Houses of Parliament, at Steyning in West Sussex, Nottingham University, at Colyton in Devon and skyped with a school in China.

Then, last year, I was on BBC1's *The Big Question* for the 75th anniversary of the liberation of Auschwitz, followed by ITV's *This Morning* and was interviewed by several radio channels. I spoke at Redditch and to over 300 young people at Ellesmere Port, Chris came over from Norway to hold my hand in what was quite an emotional time for me, at HM Prison in Leeds, Bath University's TEDx Conference, an Interfaith event at the Leeds Church Institute and one at St.

Edmund's Church, Caistor Grammar School, the Headingley Festival of Ideas as well as the York one, the Regional Conference of Rotarians in Scotland, the DWP in Leeds and many schools. I was even asked to appear on *Eggheads*.

Since I am reluctant to travel abroad, Skype conferences are getting more frequent, including with a school in Germany, a college in Brazil and many individuals, including graduate or postgraduate students, all over the world

In all, and despite some periods of illness, I managed to fulfil 43 engagements, speaking to over 7,000 people in 2015. My website gets thousands of hits too and it takes quite a bit of time trying to keep up with it and to ensure it is up-to-date.

I hope to be part of the Yorkshire Holocaust Heritage and Learning Centre to be set up at Heritage Quay in Huddersfield University, something really worthwhile and needed.

But there is life beyond the past, beyond Holocaust education. I was 92 in November 2015 and never thought it possible that I would live that long.

I take it day by day and do the best I can each one as there might not be a tomorrow. I am greatly saddened by the current refugee problem. I have been there and done that; do we ever really learn?

Irene's Story

*

Irene was my mother. But to understand her I have to go much further back.

Her parents were Isidore Elbogen (or Ellbogen or Ellenbogen) people were not too accurate at spelling of names, when registering them in those days and Netty (for Annette) Greiner.

About Isidore I know only snippets – and I do not know how true these are – except that he came to Topolcianky, where my grandparents lived, as a teacher. He was quite a character.

Grandmother's father was the local land agent so his wife was well catered for except that she had 18 children. Among them were two sets of twins and 11 of them lived to a ripe old age.

When I asked grandmother how her mother could have coped she replied: 'There was always a wet nurse.' I was about six at that time and did not realize that a wet nurse breastfed babies.

The Woman with Nine Lives

I must have been four or five when we visited the family house, where one of gran's sisters still lived. There were huge wooden gates leading into a central gravelled area. The living quarters were on the left and there were pots of red geraniums all along a veranda. They had been painted red to match the blooms.

To the right was stabling but no horses any more. Gran's sister came out with a bucket of food for the geese and called them in from the field at the back of the house. They came running. The grain was put into their beaks and massaged down their long necks. They crowded around her trying to get to her and she talked to them incessantly. I did not realize that they were being force-fed to produce fat goose livers. They seemed so keen to eat.

I was told that in the Jewish cemetery there was a section with a fancy rail around it in which all the Greiners were buried.

The young Greiner boys were a venturesome lot, not least uncle Bela, who had gone with a boat to China to trade and had started the family fortune with a paper and pulp company.

Netty was the beauty of the family and attracted the attention of Isidore, the schoolmaster. The Greiners were a religious family and told Isidore that, according to custom, Netty's hair would be shorn before the wedding.

I was told he replied: 'If you cut a single one of her hairs I shall not marry her, it is her crowning glory.' So Netty kept her shiny hair in a crown on top of her head.

My mother was born in Topolcianky but soon Isidore and Netty, with their two girls, she had a sister called Janka, moved to Bratislava. They lived in an apartment on the first floor of a large house facing the main market square. Big wooden double doors led into the inner courtyard and, at one time, horses and carriages were stabled on the ground floor. But, by now, in the 1920's the days of such transport were gone.

Grandfather had a practical mind and decided that teaching was not really a very lucrative business and that it would be wiser and also more fun to arrange for only one half of the courtyard gates to be opened and for the other to be made into a workshop where he would indulge his passion for the new-fangled fashion for bicycles.

It turned out to be a very lucrative idea and, before long, that small workshop was not big enough and a shop was rented in the city and sewing machines added.

Irene seemed to have inherited her father's go-getting attitude. After leaving school she learned shorthand and typing and became the first female court stenographer.

Post First World War inflation was such that she got paid twice a day because the morning's wages could buy a loaf of bread but by the end of it that was no longer possible. Paper money was so valueless that grandfather used it to paper the sitting room, it was cheaper than wallpaper.

I don't know how Irene and Beno met; they were married in 1921 and again, there was no question of mother's hair being cut, she retained her long, black locks, piled up on top of her head. Mother complained that the weight of her hair gave her headaches and, as fashion changed, she finished up with a modern short bob.

Irene and Beno started their married life in Kosice, where I was born. Father was the regional representative of the Assicurazione Generali. I have his original contract which even specified what furniture there should be in the office, which staff he was to appoint and what to pay them.

But by 1925 grandfather found the cycle and associated business too big to manage and he asked Beno to resign from his position and take over the running of it together with Irene.

She turned out to be a business wizard.

Mother figured that it needed to expand. Young men wanted the most modern bicycles while women needed to prepare their trousseau, so selling and repairing sewing machines should be added. Once the clientele married, they would want entertainment, especially in the villages, so there was an opportunity to sell them gramophones and records and then they would need to get more records and needles. Next, they'd have children, and could be sold baby carriages and, naturally, there would be accessories for them. And some girls would want bicycles of their own, with colourful skirt guards on the rear wheels to match their Sunday best. Mother barely took time off to give birth to Tomy in 1929.

Market research was unheard of then but mother was right. The business bloomed, we had one of the first motorcars, obviously a black Ford Model T, and mother was the first woman to pass the driving test in Bratislava. Admittedly people ran for cover when she appeared in the driving seat.

Also, unusually, the store did its own hire-purchase, so buyers could spread the cost of their consumerism. It was a good idea but when the financial crash of the '30s arrived and the government announced a moratorium on all debts, the business crashed. From then on it had to be cash only and it weathered the storm.

Those times also brought the shadow of rising Nazism in Germany. We stopped importing goods from there and now relied on Czechoslovak manufacture only. Most of the factories were in the Sudetenland and when Germany annexed it in 1938 serious supply problems arose.

But we managed, somehow, even when we had to

move from our apartment, when the business was aryanised. Mother remained a tower of strength, arranged for me to escape to Hungary, to smuggle grandmother out of the camp in Zilina and to get Beno out of the Sered concentration camp in Slovakia and all of them, in a boat to Budapest.

She and my father finished up in the immigration centre in Szabolcs utca, in Budapest and eventually in Auschwitz. Mother would never speak about her experiences and records are sparse.

She survived, got the business back and on its feet but lost it again when it was nationalised under Communism. Still, she put Tomy and Magda, her niece, through university, saw us all married and visited me frequently in England.

She also remarried in 1948. To uncle Imre, father's cousin, who had survived Auschwitz. And she became betrothed for a third time after uncle Imre's death but this marriage was a disaster.

Mother died in 1971 and is buried in Braitslava.

Cemetery in Bratislava

Aftermath

❋

When it was my 90th birthday I had a surprise visit from my niece Eva, who lives in Vienna and her daughter, Suzi, who has a house in Israel.

They knew very little of our family history so we spent a lot of time filling in gaps. They did not know of the family origins in Topolcianky. When I mentioned the place and wondered why mother had not been buried there and whether they would like to go and see the old family cemetery, they recoiled in horror.

'No Jew will ever put their feet into Topolcianky!' they said.

'Why ever not?' I asked.

'Don't you know what happened there after the war?' And then they told me.

Topolcianky had quite a large Jewish community before the war including the local doctor. He, his wife and children were taken to Auschwitz where the children perished. After Auschwitz was liberated, he returned to Topolcianky and set up again in practice.

In the late 1940s, polio became endemic but there was a vaccine now for it. The doctor offered, in memory of his children, that he would vaccinate all the young in the village without a charge. The inhabitants were curious. Why would a Jew do something for nothing, they wondered.

Would he really honour the memory of his children by saving Christians?

They talked among themselves, spoke to the local priest and somehow the idea took hold that he was not going to save the children, but kill them all, because he had lost his own.

During the night they came to his house and murdered him and his wife.

*****

EVERYWHERE I talk, the audience want to hear the poem I wrote about the Holocaust. So, as a conclusion, it is printed here. Two documents are also reproduced, the testimony of my mother sent to the Red Cross in 1961 detailing our family's suffering in the concentration camps – that document now is barely legible, but what can be read has been translated – and the card detailing the internment of my father in the concentration camp.

The Holocaust poem

I was there

Auschwitz-Birkenau - June - July 1944

Hundreds of women, their heads shorn,
In ragged clothes
Standing in rows of five, for hours and hours
In the rain, in the heat, being counted.
We are thirsty, so thirsty, but there is no water.
Thirst is worse than hunger.
Some fall down, limbs contorted
We do not dare to do more than whisper:
'Get up! You have to get up. Get up!
If you don't get up, you'll die.'
Mengele goes past, sees the fallen
Points to others to pick them up.
Where have they gone? They're never seen again.
I was there

Night time -the hut –
The girl – frantic – diabetic –
Knew she couldn't survive – no medication.
Only the healthy might survive.
Taken to the end of the hut – Doctors among us attend
her,
Talk to her – there's no hope for her.
Went into a coma, died at dawn – taken away.
I didn't even know her name, but
I was there.

The Woman with Nine Lives

Every day we stood and were counted
Again and again.
Morning, noon, evening – for hours.
Nerves stretched to breaking point
Some couldn't bear it, ran to the perimeter fence
Get stuck like spread-eagled butterflies
On a specimen board.
The fence is electrified.
This factory of death was Auschwitz – Birkenau.
I was there.

We stood, past being hungry, past being thirsty
Got thinner, feebler, more fell,
More disappeared.
Only the strong and the healthy now remained
One day we're told to strip
To hold our rags above our heads, prodded like cattle.
Don't move, moving is dangerous
It singles you out, makes you vulnerable.
The secret of survival is not to be noticed, but
I was still there.

Now Mengele asked for doctors and nurses.
To go with a labour transport.
Could we trust this evil man?
With his perverted sense of humour?
The man, who roared with laughter
When we got out of the wagon
We five, doctors and nurses, linking arms,
A scarf on the grizzled head of our aged doctor,
Hiding her in the middle – marching ahead, singing,
Through the portal which proclaimed

ARBEIT MACHT FREI – WORK GIVE YOU
FREEDOM.
But led to death.
We five are still together, supporting each other
You need friends to survive.
I was there.

Now we stepped out together, volunteering,
We knew if we stayed we would not live long
Nobody does here in Auschwitz-Birkenau.
Sooner or later you end up dead.
Gassed, ashes, made into grey coarse soap
Bits of bone sticking out
To scratch, to remind you that
You're still there.

This transport – was it real?
Or one of his jokes?
We might get out – or be sent to the gas chamber.
We took the risk   wouldn't you?
We were the fortunate few, the five hundred
Went to work in armament factories
Constantly bombed, but still alive, now living in hope.
Our hope was justified;
Our hope was their despair.
But this was not to be the end –
March in the dark
Walk and totter towards perdition,
'Don't stop, don't fall, they'll shoot you.'
I was there.

The Woman with Nine Lives

TODAY

I am here – today;
What have I learned? What do I now know?
I do know that human cruelty knows no bounds
But I still don't know why I survived, when so many
died?
Perhaps I survived – to keep the memory alive
To bear witness – to talk to you
Hoping you will listen.

So listen to me, please:
Be aware, be vigilant
Do not let differences in people
Colour, religion, ethnicity, gender or class
Be the deciding factors on how they're treated.
Differences should be valued and respected.
I am different from you – you are different from me –
But that does not make me worth less than you,
It just makes me more interesting to you
And YOU more interesting to me.

I am not going to flay you
Make a lampshade out of your skin
As they did in Auschwitz-Birkenau
To see what's under the skin
Because I know that under the skin
We are all the same.

Listen to me, please:
We all have rights and responsibilities.
The right to be heard,
The right to be listened to.

Aftermath

But we have to take responsibility
For what we are saying, what we are doing
Or failing to do.

Listen to me, please.
I have faith in you, the young people of today
That you will listen and not make those mistakes
Which led to the Holocaust
And are leading to genocide even today.

I believe that you will build bridges
Not frail ones which will break in the slightest wind
But strong, sturdy ones
Based on understanding and respect for each other
And the desire we all have
For mutual trust and genuine peace.

Remember two things, please:

Under the skin we are all the same
And   each of you can make a difference.

So do not disappoint me!

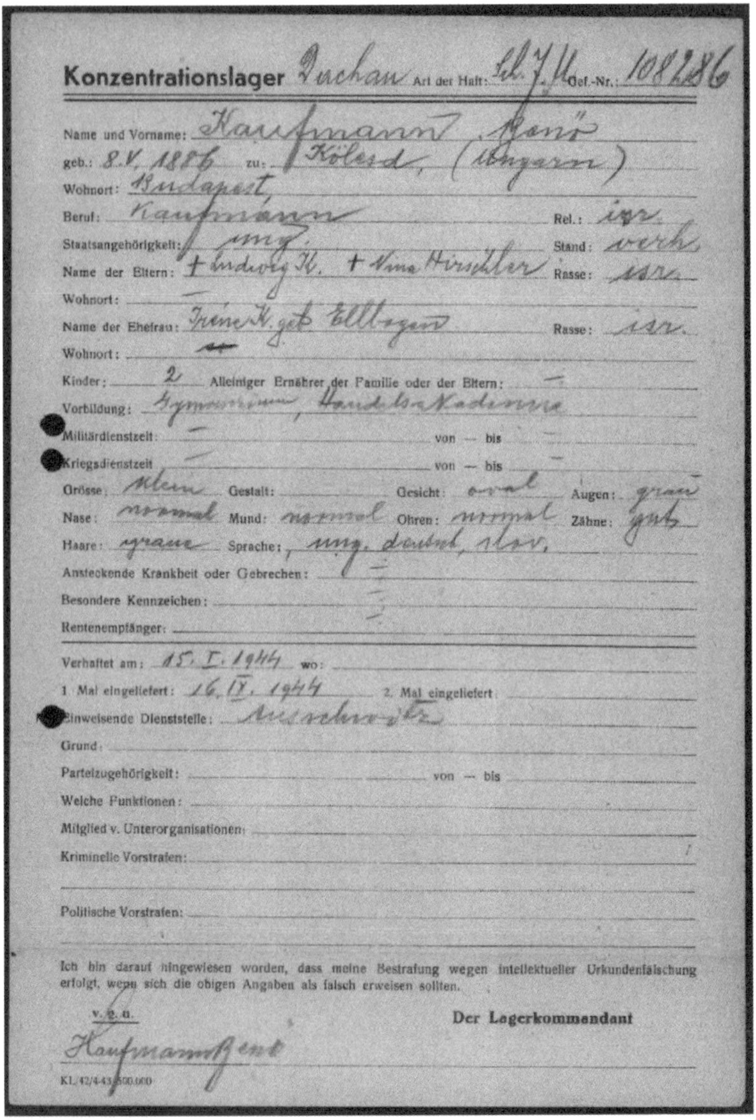
Konzentrationslager Dachau Art der Haft: Sch. J. U. Gef.-Nr.: 108286

Name und Vorname: Kaufmann, Jenő
geb.: 8.V.1886 zu: Kölesd, (Ungarn)
Wohnort: Budapest,
Beruf: Kaufmann Rel.: isr.
Staatsangehörigkeit: ung. Stand: verh.
Name der Eltern: + Ludwig K. + Nina Hirschler Rasse: isr.
Wohnort: —
Name der Ehefrau: Irene K. geb. Ellbogen Rasse: isr.
Wohnort: —
Kinder: 2 Alleiniger Ernährer der Familie oder der Eltern: —
Vorbildung: Gymnasium, Handelsakademie
Militärdienstzeit: — von — bis —
Kriegsdienstzeit — von — bis —
Grösse: klein Gestalt: Gesicht: oval Augen: grau
Nase: normal Mund: normal Ohren: normal Zähne: gut
Haare: grau Sprache: ung. deutsch, slov.
Ansteckende Krankheit oder Gebrechen: —
Besondere Kennzeichen: —
Rentenempfänger: —

Verhaftet am: 15.I.1944 wo:
1. Mal eingeliefert: 16.IV.1944 2. Mal eingeliefert:
Einweisende Dienststelle: Auschwitz
Grund:
Parteizugehörigkeit: von — bis
Welche Funktionen:
Mitglied v. Unterorganisationen:
Kriminelle Vorstrafen:

Politische Vorstrafen:

Ich bin darauf hingewiesen worden, dass meine Bestrafung wegen intellektueller Urkundenfälschung erfolgt, wenn sich die obigen Angaben als falsch erweisen sollten.

v. g. u. Der Lagerkommandant

Kaufmann Jenő

KL 42/4-43 500.000

Copy of Doc. No. 10126776#1 (1.1.6.2/KAU-KEO/00044044/0002)
in conformity with the ITS Archives
Häftlingspersonalbogen KZ Dachau

Part-translation of Mother's letter to the International Red Cross in Switzerland dated 1961

❋

For survivor victims of experiments on humans.

I request compensation for bodily and health damages which I have suffered as a victim of human research in a concentration camp in accordance with the German government regulations of 26th July 1951.

I declare that the following submission is done to the best of my knowledge and memory:

I declare that I give hereby permission to the International Red Cross to make appropriate research of the authorities or organisations involved.

The Woman with Nine Lives

<u>Personal details</u>

Family name: Foldesova born Ellbogenova Imprisoned under the name of Kaufman (or Ellenbogen)

First name: Irene

Place and date of birth: 12th December 1896, Topolcianky, District Zlate Moravac, Czechoslovakia, at present part of Slovakia

Present place of domicile: Czechoslovakia, Bratislava Palisady 51

Place and date of capture: Bratislava, Zaborska 14

I managed to smuggle my late husband out of the Sered camp and we escaped with my mother and niece and son, altogether five persons to Budapest. We came along the Danube in a boat. I became aware that those who were refugees in Hungary were then sent to Auschwitz, I have witnesses who can confirm this, their statements are in legible handwriting or were typewritten. If you require I can send these as enclosures.

Family status: Remarried in 1947

Name of spouse: Mr Imrich Foldes PHD

Date of birth: 22nd February 1889

Place of birth: Bonyhad, Hungary

Profession of spouse: Pharmacist

Children: (name, date of birth, place of birth, profession, residence)
Tomas Kaufman, 19.1.1929, Bratislava, Mechanical Engineer, Bratislava
Ibola, 25th November 1923, Kosice, Reading, UK

Citizenship of applicant:

a. At time of capture - Czechoslovakia b. At present – Slovakia

Occupation of applicant / Profession:

a. Clerk b. Profession Prior to capture - Business Manager c. Present occupation (self-employed or employed activity) - Disabled

Income of applicant: (amount of monthly net income)

a. Before capture – (illegible) b. At present - Invalidity Pension of 420 KCS per month

Attached - certificate about invalidity and old age pension of myself and my husband

15. Details of dependents of applicant
(Parents, other relatives or unmarried children, from which source and to what amount)

The Woman with Nine Lives

<u>Details of acts of violence and injury towards applicant or family members</u>

1. Type, place and duration of injury sustained –
    violation in Auschwitz. Broken ribs. Witnesses can
    confirm this. Besides that my father was in the camp
    in Zilina where he perished.
    Cause of violent treatment – I could not get quick
    enough to the Appel.
2. Stay in concentration camps, where and duration.
    From 11th July until the end of October 1944 I was
    in Auschwitz Birkenau. From November to the end
    of February 1945 in Prarschints. After some months
    we were evacuated where I worked in the sewing
    workshop, then in Chrastava, also in the workshop.
    I made gas masks. Confirmation is attached.
3. Details of personal number – 54773
4. Period in detention centre, prison or in police
    custody – (illegible)
5. Legal verdicts – reason and date of verdict – not
    applicable.
    Location of judgment, and action carried out to be
    notified.
6. Results of the above a. Damage to property, all
    furniture, clothes and valuables, as well as the
    inventory of the business. b. Damage to health – I
    have been disabled since then.
7. Were members of the family also affected? (in
    respect of which cause and which result). My father
    was taken to Zilina and there as a result of his
    experiences and without treatment for his cardiac
    condition, died. My sister and her husband were
    taken on 1st October 1942 to Auschwitz and they

were gassed. My husband was taken to a camp in Slovakia then to Auschwitz and from there to Muhldorf. My daughter was taken to Auschwitz and experienced physical and psychological damage which will remain with her for as long as she lives.

8. Detailed description of experiments, by who, when, where - give details of individual experiments

At the beginning of August 1944, they took a sample of blood from me, and Dr SS Rodo and Dr SS Mengele then injected into my thigh to see whether these would kill me. I heard then that I had been injected with typhus. During the duration of the illness I had a high temperature, shivers, pain in the location of the injection, frequently lost consciousness and I only stayed awake by willpower. Only half of us stayed alive. Afterwards they drew blood from me to use as a vaccination. I was for several months in Block 10. I asked the SS Doctor Rodo –'how come you are taking blood from Jews and using it as a serum?'

What were the consequences of the experiments? Type and duration – For a long time I had pains on the place where the injection had taken place, swollen legs.

First medical treatment after the human experiments (when, type, results and reduction of illness).

In July 1945, when I came back from the concentration camp, I was treated by Dr Guttmann,

Bratislava, also by Dr Josef Ipari in Poddunayske, Kiskupice, who is deceased. But living witnesses can also give written testimony about this.

Last medical examination (when, by which medical results, possibility of healing). On 18th December 1961 see enclosure 5. The health institute.

Were experiments done on members of the family? Place, results and grade of present reduction in earnings.

My late sister and her husband were also taken to Auschwitz and immediately gassed. I don't know the circumstances except that in October 1942 they were taken to the camp in Zilina and nobody came back from there. The same happened with all the other members of the family.

Enclosures:

a. I attach the following enclosures to support my application 1. Proof of level of disability pension 2. Level of my old age pension 3. Certified certificates by Dr Guttmann 4.Certified witness statements 5. Result of neurological findings dated 31st October 1961 6. Medical certificate dated December 1961. Altogether six enclosures totalling 13 pages.

b. Further I refer to the following witnesses (name, profession, address of witnesses and exact details which they provide witness). (Illegible) – Tel Aviv, Israel.

Signed - 25th December 1961 Bratislava – Irene Ellbogen

As notary public I certify the signature of the above Irene Foldes born Ellbogen, housewife, previously businesswoman, living in Bratislava, Palisady 51, who has proved her identity according to law.

National notary public in Bratislava, 29th December 1961, signed and stamped.

Extract from
The Woman Without
A Number

✳

There were times when we were not on Appell, queuing for food or the toilets or being walked to and from ablutions. We sat in the sun, on the ground, leaning against the walls of the hut.

Early on, we made a rule not to talk about our families – but talking and dreaming of food was permitted. Indeed, it could not be avoided. It was a favourite topic of conversation for most of us who survived. Oddly enough, we craved for very simple things – like a boiled potato or a nice, juicy apple.

One day I happened to mention that a gipsy had taught me how to read palms. I did not believe that one really could see the past and the future in the lines of a hand but it passed the time and I made sure that everybody got their allocation of at least two children, a lover or a husband, or possibly both. I explained, as it had been explained to me, what the various lines and marks on the palm represented and it became a matter of heated discussion when people found different interpretation to the same signs. I did not think that it caused any harm. Every so often, I saw a hand which gave me some concern but I always found other things to tell.

I shall never forget, however, when one day a girl,

who managed to look beautiful even with a shaved head and rags on her back and who still looked the picture of health, asked me to read her hand. It was an unusual one. I asked her how old she was. She was just sixteen. The palm was smooth with hardly any signs and an extraordinarily short lifeline. Lifelines I refused to read, unless I could see that they were very long. There was literally nothing to tell from her hand, except for an early sudden death. I made up the usual rigmarole of a husband and two children and lots of travel but kept my eye on her after that. I was uneasy.

The next Appell was one where we were told to strip, bundle our clothes and lift the bundle in both hands above our heads. People seemed to be selected at random. Mengele and a woman officer had gone along the line and we, who had not been selected, heaved a sigh of relief – when that girl suddenly sneezed. Mengele's head swivelled round, he pointed at her and signed for her to step out and join the others who had been selected. They all went into the gas chamber. I refused to read any more palms after that.

We heard of people running to the wire and being electrocuted, of those being hanged, some skinned alive and their skins used to make lampshades and of medical experiments being carried out. We never heard any good news.

I awoke one morning and could not move. My left leg felt paralysed. My friends helped me to stand up but I could not move my leg or hip nor bend it at the knee. I was in agonising pain. If I could not stand at Appell I would be sent straight away to be gassed. They called the Capo.

'There is just one chance for her' the Capo said. 'Take her to the hospital.'

My friends laid me on a blanket, picked up the four corners and started to carry me there. We met some German guards on the way. They looked, shrugged their shoulders and pointed to the hospital. My friends left me there in the care of a Czech woman doctor. She examined me and said she could not find anything organically wrong, perhaps a few days lying down might cure it. There was no medication.

The hospital was a dangerous place.

For most people there was only one way out – death – either from natural causes or as the result of experimentation. At the time, experiments were going on with X-rays. It seemed as if people were selected at random to be X-rayed – regardless of whether or not there was a need for it. It seemed random to us but probably not to the German doctor who was carrying it out. Most people were selected repeatedly to be X-rayed. I was X-rayed once but not having a number tattooed on my arm meant that they could not keep a check on me. When the German doctor asked for the woman without the number, the Czech doctor told him that I had died of meningitis. I was not the only one without a tattoo.

Every day the hospital was inspected and people who were very ill were selected and taken away, never to be seen again. There were several cases of meningitis in the hospital. The Germans thought that the disease was contagious and would not go near patients who had it or who had died from it. During the period of inspection, the Czech doctor put me into the middle of these patients – it was a relatively safe location from the Germans, but not from the disease.

After a few days my pains eased. The doctor told me that to be safe I would have to leave the hospital soon. In the meantime, I was given an armband and officially a nurse. After three days they smuggled me back to my hut. This paralysis of my left leg has occurred from time to time since then, usually before travel or in times of extreme stress.

Days later, when I didn't move quickly enough for a German soldier, he hit me with a rifle butt across the shoulders.

The Woman Without a Number

My friends and I realised that if we stayed on in Auschwitz, sooner or later one or all of us would be selected to go into the gas chamber. Lack of food and, even more, of water was weakening all of us. We decided that we would go out with the next transport which would be sent to work.

About a week later at a selective Appell, Dr Mengele asked whether there were any doctors or nurses among us.

'This is it,' I said. I was in the first line and stepped forward, to be followed by my friends. It was a risky thing to do, but we were going together – for better or worse. We were told to go to the side and to join some able-bodied women who had already been selected.

It was now the end of July 1944. We were marched away and this time it was much further than the normal showering/disinfecting block. We were herded into a large, empty room, told to strip and pushed into a shower room. By now we were used to this. After the shower we were pushed into another large room, which was divided by a long counter, behind which stood women in striped uniforms and behind them were mountains of clothes. We were told to approach the counter in fives and to move along. We were each issued with two pairs of white cotton knickers, two white cotton vests, a woollen dress, a warm woollen coat, on the back of which was a streak of yellow paint, still quite tacky, a night shift of blue gingham flannel, a towel, a piece of soap and a blanket. We were fitted with a pair of stout shoes and given a canvas bag and an enamel mug. Thus loaded we were pushed into the next room, told to dress, to put our 'belongings' in the bag.

We were given some more substantial soup than usual and then told to bed down for the night. We managed to get near to the top wall and got into our, now usual, spoon pattern to go to sleep. There was more room here than in the blocks.

Before I managed to get to sleep two young girls in striped pyjamas, aged about twelve crawled over to me. They were twins whom I had fleetingly known in Szekesfehervar. They told me that, being twins, they had not been put into the gas chamber but were being used for experiments – different substances were being injected into them. They also told me that they had seen their own parents being pushed into the gas chamber. They finished by telling me, 'You are leaving this place; you are going to live, but we are not. Once they finished experimenting on us twins, they will send us to the gas chamber. Remember what you have seen here and tell the world about it, because we will not be able to do so.'

It has taken me a long time to be able to do this.

The next morning we were given a hunk of bread and a drink of water and were then taken to the railway siding and put into cattle trucks. There was some straw there, but the guards who were going with us made us pile it up in one corner and then put their own haversacks on it. 'This is our place,' they said 'you keep well away from it.'

We did.

Eventually all 530 of us were entrained, the guards swung themselves up into the trucks and we were off. The journey took three days. The train stopped and started, went forward and backwards – there seemed to be the sound of gunfire nearly all the time. Whenever we were stopped the guard slid open the door, but warned us not to go out. Eventually he did let us go out, one by one, accompanied by a guard, to relieve ourselves. The hunk of bread we had brought with us had been eaten long ago and the half barrel in the corner, which had been full of water, was now dry. We were hungry and thirsty and so were the guards. They had also finished the rations they had brought in their haversacks.

On the second night the train stopped near a station.

The guards again opened the door. Their sergeant came from the front of the train and consulted with them. Then he walked to the station. About half an hour later big cauldrons of hot pea soup were being trundled along.

'All right,' said the guard, as he was given a beaker of soup, 'there is enough for everybody here.' So there was. Our mugs were filled with the best food we had been given since our arrival in Auschwitz.

At dawn we continued our journey. After we had shared the soup with the guards we realised that life had taken a turn for the better.

We arrived at Lippstadt on the fourth day. A camp site had been prepared for us. It was a hutment for slave labour inside a high wire enclosure. Each hut had several rooms with three-tiered bunks and, at the end of each, was a washroom with showers and long troughs with taps for washing. We five were told to go to the first hut just inside the gate: this was the hospital hut. 'Make a Revier,' was the order. In German military language a Revier was a sickbay. Since ours was not only a sickbay but also acted as a clinic, pharmacy, medical and nurses' quarters, I referred to it then, and still do, as a 'hospital'.

The first room on the left, which faced the gate, was to be our bedroom. There were two single beds and two double bunks in it, with a straw-filled mattress in each. The doctors had the single beds, we the bunks.

There were several rooms on each side of a long corridor running down the middle and the usual washing facilities at the end. The first room opposite to ours was comparatively small, so it was decided to make that the 'isolation room'. The next one was large and became the clinic. The one opposite was to be the operating theatre and the other rooms were fitted with single beds as wards.

Naturally, before anything could be done we had to have an Appell – just to check that nobody had gone missing on the journey. No, we were all there, all 530 of us. We were mostly Hungarians until a second transport of about 300 women joined us in November. In that group were women of French, Dutch, Slovak, Greek and Romanian nationality.

We were being guarded by members of the Wehrmacht, the German Army. There were a couple of female officers. The others, except for the Guard Commandant, were either very young or rather old and decrepit.

The Guard Commandant decided that there had to be a person in charge of each hut. These he picked at random from people who could speak German. I was put in charge of the hospital hut. He then told us that there was also to be one person in overall charge of us and Ella, my cousin, was chosen. That proved to be rather useful for all of us – she and I managed to finesse around the Germans on several occasions.

Next to our camp there was a huge torpedo-shaped bunker for the German officers and soldiers and slit trenches had been dug in front of our huts for us to use in case of air raids. Next to the bunker was a large factory, which produced all kinds of weaponry from hand grenades to bombs, from machine gun bullets to anti-tank weapons. On the other side of the factory were camps of Russian prisoners of war, who, contrary to the Geneva Convention, were made to work in the armament factory. The railway line on which we had arrived and which was also used to take the manufactured products away ran between our enclosure and the factory.

I was given a piece of paper and a pencil and was told to help the doctors make a list, in German, of the things we needed in the hospital – not that there was a guarantee that we would get them, as things were in short supply even for Germans.

The Woman Without a Number

I can't remember everything we got but we had an autoclave, forceps and scalpels, lint and rolls of gauze, which we made into swabs and sterilised, thermometers, temperature charts, spatulas, needles and catgut, crepe paper bandages and elastoplast as well as a pink antiseptic solution and iodine. It had been a long time since fabric bandages were seen in Germany. Medicines were mainly aspirin, codeine, cough mixtures and tannin tablets. There was also Vaseline and a couple of ointments and we had some spare blankets. But we had no hypodermic syringes until much later. We settled in. Those in the factories worked in two twelve-hour shifts, from six until six. We worked as the need arose, besides having a clinic at the end of each shift.

When the workers at the armament factory left or returned to camp there was Appell. The outgoing workers were counted first and, naturally, they had to march in fives. The incoming ones then had to line up - also in fives - and be counted back before being allowed to have food and go to bed.

The patients were only rarely counted. Even when, on the odd occasion, the Guard Commandant and one or other of the SS women came into the hospital, they would not enter the isolation room. If we offered to open the door, we were told to desist. That proved to have advantages.

At Appell the first thing the guards did was to go through the huts and make certain that there was nobody there. However, as they went from one hut to the next, there was nobody to check that someone, in dire need to relieve themselves, had not rushed back into one of the huts that had already been searched. The hut commandants were supposed to stop it, but then, we were not inhuman.

The agreement was that if that happened, the person had to remain inside because there was hell to pay if someone emerged from a hut that had already been searched. It meant that the whole Appell had to be restarted, including recall of the workers from the factory. Standing in the dark and – often – the rain, after working for twelve hours, getting wetter and hungrier was not exactly popular.

Since the guards rarely entered the hospital and the Commandant relied on me to tell him how many people were in the hospital hut, Ella and I had devised a system to make the numbers always tally.

While the guards were searching the huts the hut commandants and Ella did a preliminary count of those standing outside. She had been with the guards when they counted the workers going out, so she knew how many were supposed to be left inside the camp. Having counted everybody and while the guards were in the last hut before they came to the hospital, I called over to her in Hungarian, 'Mennyi kell?' How many do you need? The number required then became that of the patients and staff in the hospital hut. I acquired the nickname 'Mennikell', which naturally the Germans could not understand.

I spent my twenty-first birthday in the camp. It was a memorable day, one I shall never forget. Besides being forbidden to do any work and told to relax, I also received presents. Some of the girls worked in the aluminium section of the factory and they produced, from scraps, a necklace with a medallion spelling out my name. They also cut and engraved a small fat book with a spiral binding, the pages made from temperatures charts, which was the only paper we could get hold of. In it was the signature of every person in the camp. It was all miniaturised, the book was only about three centimetres by two, and one needed a magnifying glass to read the names and the messages. In the evening there was a party, a lot of singing and a birthday cake made from slices of bread, spread with margarine and jam – many must have gone without their special rations – with the requisite number of candles made of aluminium. Nobody, but nobody, not even the richest person in the world, could have had a more special birthday. I treasured the necklace and the book and took them with me everywhere, but somehow, somewhere, along my many moves in England, they both disappeared.

The guards around the camp were elderly Wehrmacht conscripts. The main gate was near to the hospital hut and I would often go over and talk to the elderly soldier who was on guard duty there. To me he seemed ancient, grey and wrinkled, small and shrunk – he was probably in his sixties. He often used to grumble, saying he could not see what the world had come to that had taken him from the office chair where he had sat through his life to stand now by a gate for a whole day. He had been happy working in the bank and well looked after by his Jewish boss. Life had been much easier then.

Sometimes he stood with his back to the gate, lit a cigarette and then put his hands behind his back for me to take it. This had to be done carefully and I had then to go quickly to the back of the hut to smoke the cigarette so that neither of us could be caught.

On my birthday, when I walked to the gate, the hand behind his back contained not one lit cigarette, but a packet of ten and a box of matches – both incredibly valuable presents. My hand-rolled cigarettes usually consisted of crepe paper bandage smoothed out and filled with chopped up leaves. It was a horrible cigarette, it made me and all other smokers cough, but it was a smoke.

By this time, air raids were frequent. If the sirens went off, the factory was evacuated. The workers came back into the camp, the Germans went into the bunker and we were supposed to go into the slit trenches which had been dug in the ground in front of the huts. Naturally, we didn't. If the weather was fine – and it usually was in the case of daytime air raids - blankets were spread on the ground outside and people sat or lay around. The Commandant stood at the entrance of the bunker and shouted and was hopping mad, but we really could not care less. If we saw any planes, we waved to them, although I don't suppose we were really seen. If we were, the airmen would have wondered why we were not in bunkers, but enjoying the sunshine. Somehow, we did not think that we were vulnerable – by now we were certain that we would live.

When the bombing raids continued during the night and the nearby towns were hit, the Commandant asked for volunteers to come and help with moving debris. If it was a nice day, many offered because it got us out from the camp, and passing bricks from one to another was not really such hard work. The main emphasis was always on getting the roadways clear. We worked alongside the German inhabitants, mainly women and children. Those of us who could speak German talked to them about how the war was going and how long it would last. I must admit that our main aim was to see the damage the allied bombers had done; we felt that the more, the nearer our day of salvation.

The only other way to get out of the camp was if someone had toothache. Then, accompanied by a guard, the person with the toothache was allowed to walk into town and visit the dentist – and bring back news into the camp. The dentist was a kind man; he often prescribed a lengthy course of treatment, which needed frequent visits to him, particularly, if the patient was pretty. I only managed one visit to the dentist; my teeth were in too good a condition. I had no fillings or cavities and that they were loose was due to malnutrition, a condition from which everybody was then suffering.

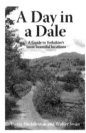

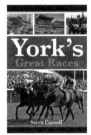

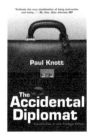

The original story of
IBY KNILL

The Woman Without A Number

The Woman Without a Number is the inspirational story of holocaust survivor Iby Knill, whose early childhood was spent in Czechoslovakia before her parents - alarmed at the persecution of Jews in Germany - smuggled her over the border to Hungary.

While there, she was caught by the Security Police, imprisoned and tortured, not just for having Jewish connections, but for being in Hungary illegally and for aiding the resistance movement. Eventually, she was sent to the infamous Auschwitz-Birkenau camp.

In June 1944, Iby left Auschwitz-Birkenau by volunteering for labour at a hospital unit. Transported to Lippstadt, she was put

in charge of a hospital and risked her life protecting the weak and helpless from the gas chambers before being freed by Allied Forces at Easter, 1945, and going on to marry a British officer.

This, then, is a truly remarkable tale that has waited sixty years to be told.

Early on the morning of his 63rd birthday, DAVE HADFIELD walked out of his front door and caught a bus...

It was the first stage in an epic journey that would take him around the furthest flung corners of his native England, showing it to him from a completely new angle.

Already acclaimed for his books on sport and music, Hadfield broadens his canvas in his finest work yet.

Heading south along the Welsh Borders, west to Land's End, along the South Coast to Dover, through London and up the eastern side of the country to Newcastle, through the Pennines and the Lakes and back home to Lancashire; he chronicles what he sees and hears on an itinerary that involves over 100 local buses.

Better still, he does it all for nothing - on a bus pass for which he was qualified by Parkinson's Disease.

Undeterred by that disability, he explores the country he loves with a keen eye and fine ear for the absurd. Thoughtful and hilarious, *Route 63* will appeal to all who have enjoyed Hadfield's writing for the *Independent*, as well as his popular previous outings.

Those new to his unique style, can discover why he has been called Bolton's answer to Bill Bryson.

The Barefoot Shepherdess

and Women of the Dales

By Yvette Huddleston & Walter Swan

The Barefoot Shepherdess and Women of the Dales celebrates the variety and versatility of a dozen or more determined women who have made a distinctive life for themselves 'far from the madding crowd'.

The Yorkshire Dales attracts tourists aplenty to appreciate the beauties of the local landscape but most visitors return to their towns and cities, renewed by the peace and quiet of the countryside, though unable to leave their modern, urban lifestyle for too long.

Women like Alison O'Neill, who owns her own flock of sheep and designs her own brand of tweed clothing, demonstrate that you can live a life of independence and fulfilment even in Britain's remotest regions. There are inevitable hardships to be endured but innumerable compensations when the Dales are on your doorstep.

Each chapter features inspirational women who have made the choice to live and work collaboratively with the people and places of the Yorkshire landscape. What they have in common - farmers, artists, vets, publicans, entrepreneurs, artisans, academics, curators and vicars - is a passion for life where Yorkshire countryside and community coincide.

Featuring personalities from the ITV series **The Dales**

Investigate our other titles and
stay up to date with all our latest releases at
www.scratchingshedpublishing.co.uk